GOING GAY

My Journey from Evangelical Christian Minister to Self-acceptance, Love, Life, and Meaning

TIM RYMEL

K Publishing

No part of this publication may be reproduced, stored in a retrieval system, or transmitted in any form or by any means, electronic, mechanical, photocopying, recording, scanning, or otherwise, without the prior written permission of the author.

Limit of Liability/Disclaimer of Warranty: While the publisher and author have used their best efforts in preparing this book, they make no representations or warranties with respect to the accuracy or completeness of the contents of this book and specifically disclaim any implied warranties of merchantability or fitness for a particular purpose. No warranty may be created or extended by sales representatives or written sales materials. The advice and strategies contained herein may not be suitable for your situation. You should consult with a professional when appropriate. Neither the publisher nor the author shall be liable for any loss of profit or any other commercial damages, including but not limited to special, incidental, consequential, personal, or other damages.

Going Gay
My Journey from Evangelical Christian Minister to Self-Acceptance, Love, Life and Meaning

By Tim Rymel
1. BIO031000 2. REL0700003. PSY016000
ISBN: 978-0-9857580-2-8

Cover design by Simone Benedettini
Interior design by Jera Publishing

Printed in the United States of America

CK Publishing
A subsidiary of Corporate Kindergarten.
Elk Grove, CA 95758
Info@CorporateKindergarten.com
CorporateKindergarten.com

Dedication

To those in the Church who hide in shame
because you are gay or lesbian

Contents

Foreword 1
Acknowledgements 5
Introduction. 9
1 Growing Up "Straight" 17
2 Don't Call It Love 37
3 The Promise of Change 51
4 My Ex-Gay Life 65
5 A New Reality. 85
6 Six Years of Silence 101
7 Love, Lust and Belonging 119
8 Giving Up 145
9 Resuming Life. 165
10 Letting Go 183
11 Self-Acceptance 201
12 Love, Life, and Meaning. 219
13 Conviction, Compromise and Compassion 233
Epilogue 247

Foreword

Struggle and Pain, Wisdom, and Nuggets of Truth

IN JANUARY OF 1990, I met Tim Rymel. He was entering the Live-in program at Love In Action. I was the Director of House Ministries at the time and was prepared to receive twelve new program members, of which Tim was a part. Our Director, Frank Worthen, spoke highly of Tim, having met him prior to his entrance into the program.

As I got to know Tim, I saw someone who was hurting and confused about life and his sexuality. I believed we held the answers that would bring him peace and joy throughout his life. I found peace with my own sexuality, was recently married, and believed I was living in God's will. I thought that the greatest joy would be found when I lived within the confines of God's standards, regardless of how I felt about it.

So I walked alongside Tim, and many others, throughout their program experiences. For over two decades I wholeheartedly believed that at Love In Action we were facilitating a program that brought God's will to men and women seeking deep transformation. We believed the process could even bring change to a person's sexual orientation.

Our belief system included the principle that any homosexual act was against the will of God, and would always bring sad and destructive consequences to the life of a Christian. Due to our convictions, we were energized to support any man or woman seeking to please God by being obedient to God's standards. What could ever be wrong with that? We often commented that it would be far better to err on the side of obedience, than to make the mistake of being too permissive. We considered ourselves to be a prophetic voice in the sea of homosexual sin. A message of freedom from homosexuality could lead men and women to satisfaction in their walks of faith and within their communities.

I was filled with a myriad of emotions as I read Tim's story. Often with tears welling up, I was reminded of the journey of my own life, and made painfully aware of details of Tim's life that I never knew. I loved Tim deeply. After he left Love in Action, I attempted to connect with him, but the phone calls were not returned. I was hurt at what had happened between us and believed Tim was so disappointed about the departure that he was angry with me and didn't want any further contact.

Then, after almost twenty years of separation, we reconnected. I discovered the reason Tim stopped returning my calls came from his own perception that he had failed as an ex-gay, and as a husband. He felt alone and lost in his secret sense of shame. I had already gone through my own transition out of ex-gay ministry. My marriage was nearing divorce. Six years of evaluation brought me to realize that the ex-gay message was deceptive, and that virtually no one experienced a change in his sexual orientation. I went through my own pain, shame and discouragement about my sexuality. I was quite surprised that Tim was going through a similar journey.

Through Tim's book, he allowed me to hear his story, which is raw, vulnerable and courageous. I could relate the struggle to my own in faith, theology, and history with the religious right. I, too, had gone through much of the same discouragement and disappointment.

I still feel regret for the message I conveyed that may have led to Tim's battle with his own sexuality and faith. I was part of the leadership of a movement that helped put shame in Tim's heart, and so many others like him. However, the fact that Tim and I are friends again shows me that we have a forgiving God that leads us with kindness into restoration. One of the most valuable messages in this book is the story of God's goodness, grace, and redemption.

You will find powerful nuggets of truth and wisdom in these pages. The chapters reveal pain, but show the struggle of a man whose face was set like flint to be a good man, and a man of integrity. You will be drawn into a captivating story leading to a powerful conclusion, in which lie the most valuable summaries. I raised my hand with a huge high five in agreement.

It's no coincidence that after two decades of separation, Tim Rymel has come to the same conclusions about life, God and relationships. This is where I see the overarching truth of faith and the kingdom of God. It hasn't lain in "correct" decisions, or the obedience to a system of dogmas and laws. Instead, God lies within the human heart just as Jesus declared.

Thank you Tim for your willingness to expose your heart through these pages. I am closer to you now than ever, because we are both living in a deeper truth and a more vulnerable existence, trusting God for the journeys of lives.

John Smid, Executive Director of Grace Rivers,
former Executive Director of Love in Action

Acknowledgements

WRITING A BOOK of this nature is really the height of self-absorption. It is sometimes painful recollection, after hours of contemplation, followed by days of reliving moments you thought were nothing but faded memories. It's life between the lines of narrative that so often become most poignant.

My partner, **Abel Perez**, has been my rock. He's ridden an emotional roller coaster he never got in line to ride. Gracefully, he took every bump, turn, twist and surprise, even patiently waiting at the top of the proverbial hill for the ride to be fixed so he could do it all over again. He has been my visionary when I couldn't see, my inspiration when I was uninspired and my faith when I had no hope. His love has been steadfast and his commitment to our relationship and our family unwavering. Without him this book (and the last one) would have remained unwritten. I am grateful to wake up every day and know that I am on a journey with someone who always has my back. No matter how difficult things become I can always count on his love and sense of humor to remind me that, "Behind every successful white man there is a Mexican."

My children, **Caity and G (Emma)**, certainly never signed up for the journey they have been on with me. I love watching them grow into the beautiful young ladies they are becoming, determined to make a difference in this world. I couldn't be any prouder of them.

My parents, **Dave and Shirley**, exemplify how true Christians should love the world around them, even when they don't understand how it all works or fits into their world view. They have always loved me and supported me no matter what stage of life or problems I've faced. They are enduring examples of kindness, patience and grace, with smiles on their faces, ready to help out whomever and wherever they can. I'm so proud to call them my parents and grateful they are my children's grandparents. I hope to be like them when I grow up.

My sister, **Judi Neifert**, who has become my best friend over the last few years, continues to show constant loving support for my family and me. I'm thankful we grew up and worked out those childhood tiffs to be the people we are today. I wouldn't trade her for any other sister. I would have when we were younger, but not now. Besides, I'm too old to start over.

Thank you to **Dr. Sean Cook**, who has demonstrated kindness, compassion, humility, and walked me through some of the most difficult experiences of my life.

John J. Smid, author of *Ex'd Out: How I Fired the Shame Committee*, and **John Paulk** have shown me how to courageously live out loud and be all that I was created to be. I'm grateful that we are a part of each other's stories and thankful to have these two men with me on the journey.

The Very Reverend Dr. Brian Baker of Trinity Episcopal Cathedral took time out of his day for a short but impactful hour to help me begin putting the pieces of my faith together again. The greatness and grace of God is truly bigger than our understanding.

The Editors

Who knew there were more rules for commas than driving instructions in a motorist's manual? Not I…or me, or whatever. My consolation for inconsistent use of punctuation is that my overly-educated editors – English majors, professors and education instructors – didn't always agree on whether or not some sentences required commas, or where they should go. I believe I speak for the general population when I say that I feel vindicated. If smart people can't agree, then the rest of us shall commit grammatical anarchy. That said, I owe a huge debt of gratitude to all those who spent hours reading and re-reading the manuscript to try to bring consistency and make sense of my ramblings. Since I have the last word (as it were) I take full responsibility for any errors present in the next few pages.

My graduate school cohort, friend, and partner in crime, **Beverly Baccala, M.P.A., M.Ed**, is still the greatest grammar police officer who ever lived. I can't thank her enough for the silly texts, emails, Facebook posts, laugh out loud side commentaries, and the cool and calm demeanor (she shows on the outside) that always says, "Everything is going to be OK." Oh, and the truffles. Everything is better with truffles.

Editor, friend and fellow author, **Dr. Christine Savi** (*Make It Happen Mantras: How to Get, Keep, and Enjoy the Ideal Job* and *How to Find, Maintain, and Enjoy Love*) constantly encourages me and treats me like a rock star, while quietly correcting my elementary errors. She always makes herself available for my stupid questions and answers them like it's the first time anyone has ever asked. I'm thankful for the brief time our paths crossed all those years ago, and the mutual sugar addiction that bonded us forever.

My fellow non-hugger, Professor **Joyce Fernandez, M.A.**, whom I love, adore and admire, all while respecting our personal boundaries, which must never be crossed unless you're a puppy. We so get each other.

Thank you to a host of pre-readers and post editors for your encouraging comments, suggestions, corrections and grammatical OCD. For good measure, I'm listing your names out of alphabetical order:

Brandi Neifert, Will Gay, Lauren Manning Gilmore, Macy Legan (you totally rock!), **Sunny Gay**, and "**Guido**" (you know who you are).

A Word to My Children's Mother

I'm thankful that God brought you into my life to share this journey. It hasn't been the voyage on the dreamboat we thought it would be, but we've shared it together. Regardless of where our lives have taken us, or will take us, you will always be a part of helping to make me a better father and a better human being.

INTRODUCTION

MY EYES OPENED around 2:00 A.M. to the sound of a crowd screaming in the background. I had fallen asleep on the sofa and was, once again, being awakened by a late-night airing of The Jerry Springer Show. No sooner did I regain consciousness than depression wrapped itself around my psyche like a tight-fitting shoe. I let out a barely audible sigh. Sleep often eluded me; insomnia was now as much a part of my routine as brushing my teeth. I slept when I could.

I hated the Jerry Springer show, but changing the channel required too much effort. "What are you going to tell our son?!" the distraught guest screamed at her husband, a transgendered cowboy who was on the show to come out to his wife and introduce his Harley-riding boyfriend. "Our son's only ten," she said, her voice growing quieter and more desperate. *How could someone do that to his kids?* I thought. *And why on national TV?* As I watched her bury her head in her hands, shaking with sobs, a tear formed in the corner of my own eye and slowly drifted over the bridge of my nose. With my own divorce imminent, my emotions were raw.

It had only been a couple of months since my wife told me our marriage was over. We had been married for six and a half years and, though our marriage was rocky from the start, I never expected to be in this situation. I made a commitment for life. In addition, the thought of not seeing my daughters every day, putting them to bed at night and waking them up in the morning, was more than I could bear. I was devastated.

Another roar from the raucous Springer crowd brought my attention back to the television. The husband's cocky attitude made me angry. I didn't know if the story was real, but my heart ached for his little boy just the same. This man projected the self-centered callousness I saw in my wife. I hated him. I hated her. I mustered the strength to find the remote and press the power button. The screen went dark.

For the next six years, I tried to make sense of my life. I went to work and I came home. With their mother chasing new relationships, I had my children with me a substantial amount of time, and I did all of the things a single parent does. Cooking, cleaning, laundry, and bedtime stories kept me sufficiently occupied to ease the emotional pain.

When I was alone, however, my small house became enormous and empty. I spent many nights on the phone with my father who patiently listened to me ramble, telling the same story, sharing the same emotions, bitterly complaining and coming to no conclusions. I was trying to understand what had happened. Anger and resentment consumed me. At night I often imagined lying in bed with a gun, putting it to my head and pulling the trigger. This scenario brought comfort in a strange way, allowing me to drift off to sleep, if only for a few hours of solace.

I was a man of deep faith. When I was younger I attended Bible School and became an ordained evangelical Christian minister. I grew up in the emotion-filled Pentecostal faith. My grandfather was an itinerant preacher and my father worked in youth and prison ministries. What I saw and heard frequently conflicted with my analytical tendencies, but I shoved my questions aside and told myself, "God has a plan. His ways are higher than my ways. I don't need to understand, I just need to trust Him."

But now I couldn't wrap my brain around that plan. I couldn't see beyond the situation. How could I make sense of a family ripped apart by adults unwilling to take responsibility and make a relationship work? Where was God in this? Why would He allow this to happen? Reality became bigger than the answers my faith could provide.

Oddly, it *wasn't* my struggle with homosexuality that sent me on a journey for answers. I had been able to suppress my sexuality for a greater cause, at least for a few years. But when I started questioning one thing, I began to question everything.

I started writing this book because it was cathartic and therapeutic. I had run from my past for nearly 20 years. I put blogs together to share my experiences, which helped me uncover and address my shame, and I found I wasn't alone. There were others. More and more Christians, and former Christians, began crossing my path. They, too, were trying to make sense of their sexual orientation and their faith. I realized I stood in a unique position: I was a formerly ordained evangelical Christian now identifying, at least on some level, as a gay man. I wasn't too far removed from one and not quite embracing the other. I belonged to two groups with viewpoints as opposed as the north and south poles. Both points of view reverberated simultaneously in my head.

Another unusual perspective I hold is that of a "success" story of the ex-gay movement. The ex-gay movement began as a religious coalition in 1976 under the umbrella organization, Exodus International. Its promise was to eliminate same sex attraction through prayer, Bible reading and the practice of "heterosexual mannerisms." I worked as a leader in the movement from 1991 to 1996 as the Outreach Director of Love in Action, one of the oldest and most renowned ex-gay ministries at the time. We had one of the only live-in programs in the world, which I attended in 1990.

While serving as the Outreach Director I had the privilege of speaking around the country in schools, colleges, and churches. I appeared on over 30 radio and television shows with the message of "Freedom from homosexuality through Jesus Christ." That was Love in Action's slogan. I presented at Exodus International conferences and even helped pioneer ministry to youth struggling with homosexuality. The 1990s were pervaded by a cultural war between the Christian right (an increasingly politically powerful coalition of protestant fundamentalists) and the gay community. I was on the front lines, working with some of the biggest names in the movement. I believed, with all my heart, in the message we delivered.

But life has a way of leading us down paths we never intended to go. Life is not handed to us in a nicely wrapped package. It seldom takes us on a linear path, or drops us off at a swanky retirement villa in Palm Springs at the end. It's one thing to accept your circumstance, but another thing to accept yourself. My journey into self-acceptance as a gay man has been a long one. I can safely say it's not over. What I offer on these pages is a snapshot of where I've been and how I got here. It's a question I'm asked frequently by Christians with whom I've worked closely in the faith, or Christian friends who simply can't understand how someone could "just give up because things aren't going your way."

We've entered a new era. With the closing of Exodus International in 2013 and popular culture's shift in its view of homosexuality, dialogue is more important than ever. Many Christians are afraid that allowing active homosexuals in their churches means allowing false doctrines and immorality, or abandoning the faith altogether. They might argue that doctrine, like the laws of physics, cannot be tampered with without unspeakable calamity. If homosexuals are allowed to enter, and partake in the Church, the floodgates of sin and immorality will be unstoppable.

Many members of the gay community, on the other hand, look at the Church with disgust and resentment. They see the Evangelical Church as a political powerhouse determined to keep them oppressed like African-Americans in the unsavory parts of our history. They see the Church as archaic in thought and sadistic in action. They can't understand why, through no fault of their own, they are outcasts and viewed as degenerates when they are simply following the same laws of nature as that of their heterosexual counterparts. The Church, of course, has found itself on shakier and shakier ground, with the divorce rate of its members equal to those without religious ties, and the occasional celebrated pastor outed as gay.

If I've learned anything over the years, I've learned that people are people are people. Neither a title nor a label nor a religious affiliation makes us any different from anyone else. Associating ourselves with a political party, a culture or a religion comes with a set of ideals to which we try to adhere. Authenticity disappears when we become more concerned about maintaining the ideal than being honest with those around us. I've seen this happen with the religious and non-religious alike.

My goal in the following pages is to give an honest glimpse into the life - the pain, the journey and the intense shame – of a Christian struggling to reconcile his sexual orientation with his faith. There are many stories like mine. They are not all the same, but they are all worth hearing.

At the same time I hope to create a dialogue between the Evangelical Christian and gay communities that allows people to have their own experiences and walk their own journeys without judgment or fear. When we humanize each other, we recognize our own shortcomings, fears, and need for love and acceptance, and it becomes difficult to point fingers and make blanket accusations. Having lived on both sides of this issue, I assure you we are more alike than we are different. Even the biggest of philosophical chasms have common ground and leave room for open, honest discussion and reconciliation.

I realize there will be those in the Church who will never accept homosexuality as a natural part of human existence, let alone as part of Christianity. Some might say I was never a Christian in the first place. There were some in the gay community, when I was a leader in the ex-gay ministry, who told me I was never gay in the first place. My point is not to argue for or against Christianity, but simply to tell the story.

Someone once said that we are "unique, just like everybody else." It's what unites us as human beings. The reason we all need each other is because we experience the world as individuals with distinct perspectives. No one is exactly like us, or sees the world exactly the way we do. We are uniquely and wonderfully made, or evolved, depending on your point of view. When we learn to accept and respect people, taking their experiences at face value and look for similarities, we stop making judgments and find common ground.

> *"For now we see only a reflection as in a mirror; then we shall see face to face. Now I know in part; then I shall know fully, even as I am fully known. And now these three remain: faith, hope and love. But the greatest of these is love."* 1 Corinthians 13:12-13 (NIV)

— I —
GROWING UP "STRAIGHT"

FOR SOME REASON I vividly remember, at 11 years old, standing in my parents' kitchen with my friends. We were talking about a new girl at school to whom all the boys were attracted. "She's mine!" said my friend Joey.

"No, she's *my* girlfriend," bantered another friend.

I looked around the table at the other boys who genuinely seemed interested in this girl. *I don't feel anything for her*, I thought. *Maybe they don't feel anything either and this is just what we're supposed to do.* "Well, I'm going to ask her out first," I said with a little less confidence than my friends. We laughed and went on with our day, playing cops and robbers, trucks, and GI Joes, just like 11-year-old boys do.

I spent much of my life thinking, *Maybe this is what I'm supposed to do. Maybe that's how I should feel.* I took social cues from family and friends. It never dawned on me to ask or talk about my feelings. Feelings were always nebulous. I learned that, to keep from making waves at home or school, I had to curb my reactions and often suppress how I truly felt. I made observations about how other people felt and subsequent determinations about how I was supposed to act.

In the '70s, my knowledge of homosexuality was limited to occasional slurs from my father when gay rights parades came on the news. It was the era of Anita Bryant and pre-AIDS. The American Psychological Association didn't remove homosexuality as a disorder until 1973, just three years before my first realization that I might be different than the other boys. The battle for gay rights had only recently begun to ignite. As far as my parents were concerned, of course, it wasn't a relevant issue in our house.

Joey was one of my neighbors and best friends. Joey's mom was on her third marriage. His step-dad was devoutly Mormon and I knew little more about his life than that. Years later I found out that his mom hit on my dad by asking him to come over and look at her water heater while her husband was at work. At the time, however, I saw Joey's home life as much more stable than it actually was.

As we entered puberty we talked about our body parts as all developing boys do. I was a late bloomer and had yet to experience full-on sexual attraction, but I was drawn to Joey's blonde hair and blue eyes. I didn't know what it meant, but I knew I wanted to be around him.

"Let's play truth or dare," Joey suggested one night at a sleepover at my house. We had built a fort in my backyard and decided to spend the night in it. The flimsy building was made of plywood, 2x4's and nails we managed to hammer in only deep enough to hold the pieces together. It wasn't much, but we had done it by ourselves.

"Ok," I said. "What's that?"

"It's where I ask you 'truth or dare' and you either have to tell me the truth about a question I ask, or do what I dare you to do." I was naïve enough that I couldn't imagine what he would ask me to do that might be uncomfortable. I had nothing to hide at that age.

Our game started innocently enough, but Joey's questions became more sexual in nature, asking me to touch him or let him touch me. I liked the attention and the touching felt good. Joey talked about masturbation, which I had not yet experimented with, but it sounded like a great idea. Eventually, we grew tired, turned off the flashlights and went to sleep.

The next day Joey asked me to come over to his house and help with some chores his mom asked him to do. "Come on, faggot, help me rake these leaves," Joey said. I laughed uncomfortably, not really understanding the context. "We're fags, you know," he said. At this point he was laughing, too.

I knew he was just joking with me, but the joke was awkwardly uncomfortable. I connected the dots. We were both boys and we had touched each other the night before. I remembered hearing my father use the term fag, but I thought it just referred to guys who *acted* like girls. The way Joey used the term didn't really fit the way I understood it. Either way, it was a negative term and I knew I didn't want to be associated with it. I didn't respond to Joey's comments; I simply tucked the experience away.

Joey didn't get along with my next-door neighbor, Tommy, and I was often caught in the middle of their fights, forced to choose sides. We were all roughly the same age and entering puberty at nearly the same rate. My friends started talking more about girls, but that interest never materialized for me. I kept offering to play "truth or dare," but was turned down more and more frequently. It started to feel awkward even bringing it up.

Whatever confidence I'd had in grade school was stolen by puberty and replaced with acne, braces and headgear. I entered seventh grade looking and feeling like a nerd. Fortunately, I met a new friend, Brian, who oddly became somewhat of a mentor to me. We grew up on opposite sides of the tracks. I saw him as my Fonzie, the cool guy from a popular TV show called Happy Days that was on when I was a kid. Brian was confident, direct and able to talk to anyone. He was also a smoker at the ripe old age of 12. Even now, when I envision Brian, I remember him looking like a full-grown man. Brian watched out for me. Perhaps it was the idea that we were both misfits that drew me to him. I was never attracted to Brian, but tried to emulate his "coolness." He was the only friend I had in junior high who also changed schools with me when my family moved right before eighth grade. I lost connection with all of my childhood friends by that point. Then Brian's family moved away while we were in the middle of eighth grade. I was about to enter high school, which again was new, and the people I'd grown accustomed to seeing would not be there. I felt very much alone and disconnected.

According to my parents, I was an outgoing child, quick to make people laugh. I come by that honestly; it's a family trait. I didn't have problems talking to strangers or making new friends. Around 12-years-old, that comfort with strangers was replaced with self-consciousness and the feeling that I was different.

As puberty hit full bloom, my pull toward guys turned into genuine sexual attraction, but it wasn't until I was a freshman in high school that I made the connection to homosexuality. I don't think I'll ever forget it. I was standing in my mother's kitchen when a wave of panic swept over me. The feeling-turned-thought reverberated inside my body. *I am a fag*, I thought. My heart raced. I felt sick. I could never share this with anyone, least of all my parents. I knew, even then, I didn't want to be gay; I wanted to be "normal."

I was filled with anxiety and wondered how to get rid of my sexual feelings. I wasn't sure what this meant in the long-term. I knew, however, it was something to be ashamed of and that it must remain hidden. I wondered if I would be attracted to guys all my life, or if it would eventually go away.

Even at 14 I pictured myself one day married with a wife and children. Both of my parents came from large families. My grandmother married at 13, had 2 children, divorced around 17 and married my grandfather, with whom she produced 16 more children. I didn't know anything but a traditional family life. I certainly didn't have role models for gay relationships. No other options ever entered my mind. I kept my secret throughout high school, which is also when I began to experience more intense anxiety.

I was a good-looking kid with very low self-esteem. I felt ashamed and embarrassed most of the time, though I didn't know why. It didn't take much for me to turn beet red. On my first day of high school, for example, I asked my English teacher a question after class when I was sure no one else was around. Then, later that day, I had the same teacher for another subject.

"Before I forget…" he said, "Someone asked me a great question in my first period class that applies to all my classes. In fact he's sitting…" he paused and made eye contact with me. My heart sank into my stomach and I must have turned completely pale at the prospect of being called out, because he quickly looked away. "Well… it doesn't matter who asked," he finished. Attention mortified me.

I managed to make friends with two other misfits in the high school. Looking back now, one was obviously gay and the other was self-consciously overweight. None of us had friends except for each other. The others were bullied occasionally, but I wasn't. I had learned to stay under the radar by keeping to myself and staying out of the way. Of course, puberty is bad enough for anyone, but throw in same-sex attraction on an insecure kid with headgear and it's practically unbearable.

"Hey," Renee, one of the more popular kids, said to me in class once. "What do you think of my lipstick?" She caught me off guard. I felt like everyone was suddenly looking at me.

"Looks good," I said quietly, shrinking down in my chair.

"I always thought I had chicken lips," she said. "It's hard to put lipstick on a chicken." She made me smile.

"Why are you talking to him?" her friend asked her.

"Because he always sits there quietly and doesn't say anything. I was trying to bring him into the conversation." My smile melted into embarrassment as my face grew hot. I appreciated the gesture and wished I could come out of my shell, but doing so was too much of a risk. I didn't want to be found out for who, or what, I really was. Even I didn't know.

My father was an angry man when I was younger. His style of parenting involved yelling, name-calling, and condescension. He expected his demands to be carried out perfectly and I failed him miserably. My plan of escape was to hide, sometimes disappearing to the shed in the backyard to cry, and wait, either for everything to calm down or for someone to come and find me. Some days I simply wished I could disappear and go through life unnoticed. I literally had dreams of flying away into obscurity.

When I was born my parents were attending a little Pentecostal Church of God. I don't have a lot of memories of the church because we moved to Sacramento when I was six and joined the more "sophisticated" Assemblies of God. I do, however, remember falling asleep on the pew amid shouts of praise, people running in the aisles, women who were "slain in the Spirit" during altar calls, and spirited Southern Gospel quartets. Emotion was synonymous with a relationship with God. In fact, it was preached, if you didn't feel God you weren't having an experience with God and there was something sinful about you. This would mess with my head years later, as I grew to become more and more of an analytical person.

As a teenager, home life was difficult. My father was reeling from the premature death of his brother, who was his closest friend. His doubts about God, at that time, took us out of church. He began to drink heavily. My older sister's hormones were in full bloom and between her angry outbursts, my father's new lifestyle and my self-doubt, I longed for the peace I remembered so clearly in our family when we were involved in church.

In the summer of 1981, I went to stay with relatives to escape the chaos. My cousins and their parents attended another Assemblies of God Church. I went with the intention of committing my life to Christ on one of the weekends I was there. The youth pastors, Rob and Sherry, gave an altar call in Sunday school on one particular Sunday. "I feel like there's someone here who needs to give his heart to God this morning," Rob said. He scanned the room and our eyes made contact. I quickly looked away. Unlike my past experiences with God in church, this one wasn't particularly emotional. It was more like fulfilling an obligation I knew was good for me, like eating all the lima beans on my plate.

To alleviate some of my obvious discomfort, Rob asked all the kids to stand up and come to the front of the classroom. "Sherry and I want to pray for each of you before you're dismissed. If you feel like

God is tugging on your heart and you want to make a commitment, please let one of us know."

I let them pray for me, but I never said a word. I silently prayed, "God, I need You to take control of my family again and I need to surrender my life to You. Do what You want with me. I just want to feel Your peace in our family." Later I confessed to my cousin what I had done. He in turn told the youth pastors. I felt encouraged because I'd made a connection with God. I believed that God was in control and that ultimately He would bring my family back to Him. Still, the thought of going home was difficult. I didn't know how long it would take for God to do something and I didn't know if my parents would accept my newfound faith in light of the struggle with theirs.

"You can't stay here forever," my aunt told me. "At some point you're going to need to go back and deal with your problems." I knew she was right. I mentally prepared myself for facing the problems that plagued my family.

Upon returning home I found a church within walking distance from my house. I intended to keep my commitment to God and I did. I immersed myself in church, attending Sunday morning services, Sunday night services, Wednesday night youth, and Bible studies. It was difficult at first, because I didn't know anyone and internalized the shame I felt for simply being me. I simultaneously found solace in God's grace and believed that He loved me unconditionally, but also felt trapped by the sin that enveloped me. When I found my way into the music program, however, relationships began to click.

I had a natural propensity for music. Though I didn't start playing piano until I was 13, late by most standards, it came quickly and easily. I played by ear and learned riffs and scales by listening to

Southern Gospel albums. This skill served me well. It earned me recognition and validation. I craved both.

Edith, our church's official piano player liked me. "I don't always want to play," she said. "Would you mind filling in for me once in a while?" I wasn't sure how old she was, but at 15 I would have guessed her age to be around 103. I managed to master her style and play exactly like her. I wasn't necessarily trying, but it helped me disappear into the background while being on stage. I was too insecure to be myself. Edith asked me to play more frequently and eventually we were on a rotation schedule.

Our church services were decidedly Pentecostal. They were exactly what I remembered from the first church I'd attended as a child, the Pentecostal Tabernacle in Salinas, California. The music was loud and the shouting and prayers were louder. I was stoic, but my music was not. Music was my emotions when my body felt nothing. It was my connection to God when I felt disconnected. Music became another side of my personality, one that expressed love, openness, and vulnerability. It eventually helped me develop a stage persona, someone that I could never be without it.

In one particular service it seemed that God was determined to get our attention. The pastor preached with intensity and fervor and the congregation responded in kind. As I started to play the piano that night it felt as if something, or someone, had taken over. I played with a new rhythm I'd never played with before. It was in those moments, and many more that followed, that I felt so close to God and felt my calling. Soon I was immersed in choirs and worship teams and was even asked to play in other churches. I'd found a place to belong. Years later someone commented that when I played the piano I became a different person, more confident and sure.

Still, my abnormal attraction to the same gender ate at me. I became more involved with Bible studies to alleviate the pain, but instead, the studies only confirmed that there was something very wrong with me. My sin was much deeper than others' sins, I'd concluded. Mine was abhorrent to God. He despised it, and probably even despised me. I had no explanation for why He anointed my music or why my talent continued to grow.

In desperation I shared my secret with an adult friend at church. "We all have sin," he said in an attempt to make me feel better about myself. Marvin was a great guy. He was the maintenance man at church and worked with youth. He had a young daughter and had recently gone through a divorce. Marvin believed divorce was a sin, as we all did in our faith, and he became very accepting of others and their situations because of his own. Confessing my deep, dark secret to Marvin made me feel a little better, but I felt like I needed to do more.

Cary was our youth pastor and, though he was not particularly good-looking, I found him very attractive. It was probably his personality, position of authority, and kind words more than anything else. I volunteered to help with the youth group and found reasons to be at church. Cary was a gifted speaker and he and I worked well together in the services. I became one of the many people taken in by his charisma and constantly sought Cary's attention.

One day, while just hanging out at church, I worked up the nerve to go talk to him about my secret. I knew I was taking a huge risk, but I was desperate for answers to this unnatural attraction for other boys. Cary didn't react to my confession.

"God loves you, Tim," he said compassionately. "The Bible is very clear about homosexuality. 1 Corinthians 6:9-11 tells us that 'neither the sexually immoral nor idolaters nor adulterers nor men who have sex with men…will enter the kingdom of heaven,' but as long as you confess your sins to God, He forgives you and will help you to make the right choices. Just keep praying and ask God to reveal Himself to you. Also, you need to keep yourself covered in the Word. The devil will try to get a foothold any way he can."

Again, I felt better after my secret was shared with the youth pastor, but still found no ultimate relief. Cary never brought up the issue again. While I continued to pray and ask God for healing from my sin, I learned to separate my two passions, God and sex, into neatly organized compartments. The ongoing conflict resulted in intense anxiety and depression, running themes throughout much of my life. I was plagued by fears of dying, losing my parents to death and an overall feeling of loss of control. My health took a hit even as a teenager. Already painfully thin, I didn't have much of an appetite. At 5'10" I had dropped to 115 pounds and struggled to keep weight on.

I graduated from high school mid-term and didn't bother to go back for graduation day. I'd earned the diploma and I didn't see the need to walk down the aisle with those kids who made me feel so uncomfortable. The thought of wearing a hat and gown and having my named called out in front of the entire school was overwhelming. Anyway, I had friends in church. For the time being, I'd found a place to belong among people who admired me and my talent.

My two worlds

Back in the '80s, when video rentals were new, I wandered into a video store close to home and saw the store had a selection of X-rated videos in the back. I looked around the store to see if anyone was watching me, then made my way through the curtain to see what was inside. My heart was pounding, my hormones were racing, and I felt my face begin to burn. My desire to watch an x-rated video was matched only by my embarrassment at the idea of renting it. Besides, I didn't have a video rental card. I'd always used my parents'. I couldn't rent one of those videos with their card because they would find out and that would be humiliating. I also didn't have a credit card of my own, something I needed to get a membership at the video store.

I had received credit card offers in the mail, as I had recently turned 18, but hadn't seen a need for one. Until now. I knew it wouldn't be long before I'd get another offer and, sure enough, within the next couple of days I received the application. I quickly filled it out and returned it.

A few weeks later my credit card arrived in the mail. That same day I headed back to the video store and opened my own account. It was too soon to turn around and walk into the "adults only" section of the store. That would be too obvious. I rented a benign video for my first purchase and headed home. I'm not even sure I watched it.

As soon as the video store opened the next day I returned my previous rental and casually made my way to the adult videos hidden along the wall in the back of the store. Again, my heart was pounding. This time, however, I was determined. I had mentally worked up to this moment. I took a deep breath, looked around the store to make sure no one was watching, and I walked through the curtain. The titles were ridiculous, and each video looked like the next. I saw a small portion of gay videos in the corner, but I didn't have the nerve to check one out. For fear of being thought a pervert for staying behind the curtain too long, I grabbed a video and made my way to the counter. As chance would have it, a customer came from nowhere, jumped in front of me and began asking questions of the cashier. I stood there with a pornographic video in my hand, trying to hide the cover. *Good grief!* I mentally shouted to the customer, *They don't have your stupid video. Move!* I was almost home free.

The customer in front of me eventually got all of his questions answered and it was my turn to step up to the register. I didn't want to make eye contact with the cashier so I slyly put the video on the counter and pulled out my rental card. He picked up the video, looked at me and said, "Do you have a Beta machine?"

He's asking questions! He's asking questions! I panicked. "No," I choked.

"Well, this is the wrong one. Hang on, I'll go back and get the right one." He left me standing at the counter. I felt like a puppy that had been caught chewing up the couch cushion and was waiting to be scolded. This wasn't an interchange I'd intended to have. I watched him go behind the curtain where I knew he was going to see all those dirty videos. My confidence melted and I just wanted to leave.

"Here you go," he said, walking back behind the counter. He rang up my purchase and handed me the video. I had done it. Mission accomplished.

The experience was exhilarating. It felt wrong, but good. I had entered a world that would become my escape for the next several years, which would be marked by excitement and shame. It was my secret place. A place I would vow multiple times before God to never go again, but would inevitably return.

College Life

After graduating high school, I attended the local junior college where I earned a degree in liberal arts. I fought my father over having to attend a junior college. I was destined for Bible School and determined to become a minister. He had the foresight to tell me I needed to get my associates degree before going to a university. "Besides," he said, "I'm not paying all that money for a bachelor's degree when you can get your associates degree for almost nothing." I struggled through junior college because I had no interest in general education. I couldn't see how it was relevant in any way to my Christian faith. God was all the truth that I needed. The knowledge I would gain at a secular college was irrelevant to what I would learn in Bible school.

Many of my instructors were anti-Christian and didn't bother to hide it. "If anyone turns in a paper about Christianity or the Bible you'll receive an instant F!" touted my English professor. She liked me because my papers made her laugh. I figured out a way to work church experiences into them with a twist of humor and squeeze an A out of her. I took on the challenge with all of my instructors. With every assignment I did my Christian duty to evangelize the community college professors. I just knew I could make them see my Bible ways were right. In hindsight, of course, I don't think I made much difference. I doubt they even noticed.

My life had become rigid. Business casual was my daily wear. I felt an overwhelming need to look and act like the Christian I was supposed to be. I kept my surroundings as clean as could be and worked diligently to prove, if only to myself, that I was a good person. The only time I got into trouble for coming home late was once when my Bible study and prayer time went several hours over.

This was in sharp contrast to my sister's active social life. My parents were only worried about me getting home safely, not about what I was doing.

I continued to attend every church service, as well as extracurricular Bible studies, and memorize Scriptures. The mental fight was exhausting, but I felt it was the right thing to do. After all, God entrusted me with this "thorn in the flesh" because He knew I could handle it. I wasn't going to let Him, or my parents, down. I practiced, and learned to compartmentalize my secret life from my public life.

In 1986, after graduating with my associate's degree, I took off for Southern California. I attended Pacific Christian University to work toward a degree in Bible as a preaching major. I joined a choir in college and became one of the lead musicians and singers. Though I had committed to staying away from adult bookstores, especially since I was in Bible school, it wasn't long before I drove around town and found them all. Whenever I felt stressed or in the mood, I jumped in my car and drove to the nearest bookstore to browse through their videos and maybe buy a magazine or two. I had a private dorm room during my first semester, so I didn't have to worry about anyone finding my stash.

Unfortunately, that private room didn't stop the guilt that consumed me. I'd always end up throwing away the magazines and videos the same night, slinking out of my room to look for a dumpster somewhere off campus or out of the way where no one could link the sinful paraphernalia back to me. That activity was followed by hours of mentally beating myself up, praying for God to forgive me, and crying tears of remorse.

It shouldn't have come as a shock to me, considering what *I* did in my free time, but I was horrified to learn that some of the other preaching majors were caught getting drunk and having sex with girls. I didn't hide my disgust when their filthy lifestyles were revealed. My friend Bob, a fellow preaching major, and I discussed their activities at length, shaking our heads and questioning their choices. "Why bother to go to Bible school?" we'd ask each other. "And to be a preaching major of all things," I'd say. I pitied the churches they would eventually pastor and reviled the hypocrisy they embodied.

While at school, I met Lisa through a mutual friend. Lisa was a music major at nearby California State University Fullerton. She could sing anything from classical to pop to Gospel. She was an attractive girl, was dating one of the football players, and had a lofty goal to attend Julliard. She certainly had the talent to do so.

Lisa and I started a band with some musician friends and soon we were traveling around Southern California singing in churches. Whatever relationship I had imagined would develop between us never materialized. I had to face the fact that I just wasn't attracted to her physically, though I wanted to be. She never showed any interest in me either. Our bond plateaued to a platonic friendship and, shortly after, fizzled into nothing. The fantasy of the relationship did, at least, make me think I was more like the other guys.

Out of our time together, however, I got the professional musician bug and decided that ultimately I wanted to dedicate my life to the Christian music scene. After a year of Bible school I left Southern California and moved back home. I had concentrated so much on music that my other grades had taken a hit: A's in music, but C's, D's and F's in theology. It wasn't quite the stellar year or launch pad into ministry that I'd planned.

I had mixed feelings about leaving L.A. It was nice to be on my own and out from the under the mental stress of seeking my parents' approval. Sacramento seemed like a dead-end town, but I had nowhere else to go. My home church, upon hearing that I was available, asked me to come back and work as their music minister. I accepted the job with the understanding that I would continue my education through the Assemblies of God and work toward becoming a credentialed minister. That, as it turned out, came with its own unexpected twist.

A Rocky Beginning

Pastor Glenn, looking rather somber, called me into his office. "Tim, Pastor Steve Schneider has gone before the district board and made accusations that you are a male prostitute. The Board is denying your credentials."

I was speechless. Pastor Schneider was the pastor of the first church I attended after giving my life to Christ. The youth pastor there was Cary, to whom I had confided my secret. As far as I knew, he and Cary never had a conversation about me. Unfortunately, the Assemblies of God had defrocked Cary, the only person I could call in my defense, because after leaving our church he divorced his wife. In the eyes of the Assemblies of God, that act deemed Cary unreliable.

The only other mention of my struggle to Pastor Schneider had happened at one especially vulnerable moment many years earlier. After a particularly moving morning service I went to the front of the church and asked him to pray for me. I briefly explained that I struggled with homosexuality. Pastor Schneider put his hand on my head, tightly closed his eyes, and prayed God would take the demon out of me. After several moments of praying in tongues, he took his hand off of me, smiled at his job well done and shook my hand. It had all happened so quickly, so many years ago, I didn't think he even remembered.

"I'll set up a meeting with the district council and then we'll go talk with them and fight the accusations." Pastor Glen told me, "Steve Schneider has earned a bit of a reputation for not being quite accurate about everything he says. You'll be OK."

Several weeks later we drove to the district council's headquarters for the meeting. "Hi, Tim. How are you?" Pastor Schneider offered his hand to me as I walked through the doors of the reception area.

He is awfully friendly for a man who is trying derail my career, I thought. "I'm good. How are you?" I asked. I didn't really want to know. I was scared to death about what might come out in this meeting. At this point I'd had a chance to process everything and "male prostitute" was so far removed from anything I'd ever said to him or the youth pastor I didn't now what to expect. Even at the age of 22 I wasn't exactly sure I knew what a male prostitute was.

"Oh, you know, I'm good. Just getting older." He grinned, bearing those familiar crooked front teeth.

We sat quietly for a few more minutes without talking. My pastor had gone through the doors to meet with the council before Pastor Schneider and I came in. The uncomfortable moments felt like eternity. Finally, we were called in. We sat around a large table. Everyone wore suits and ties except Pastor Schneider and me. I, again, was always in business casual. He wore something from the 1970s, so out of touch it made him look like a recluse.

"So, Pastor Schneider," one of the elders addressed him, "you've made some pretty hefty statements about this young man. Would you like to explain yourself?"

"Well, when Tim was younger he went to see our youth pastor, Cary Cornell, and confessed to him that he was a male prostitute. As soon as Tim left, Cary came right into my office and told me what he had said," Pastor Schneider explained.

"I never told Cary that." I countered. "That conversation never happened." I wasn't willing to share the conversation that *did* happen.

"You did." Pastor Schneider held his ground.

We bickered back and forth for a few moments before one of the elders stepped in. "It appears to us that there are some unresolved issues between the two of you. Pastor Glenn has vouched for Tim's character so we're going to approve his credentialing, but we highly recommend the two of you get together outside of this meeting and work out your differences."

That's it?! I thought. This man had tried to destroy my career with false accusations and there was no punishment? I was certainly happy to receive my credentialing as an Assemblies of God minister, but it made me question the efficacy of the leadership. They seemed to stand with their own when the chips were down and, at that moment, I felt like an outsider. Nevertheless, I was afraid if I pursued justice, my real secret would be revealed. I couldn't take the chance.

Pastor Schneider and I met the following week in his office. "I'm really sorry for the misunderstanding," he said, though he never took responsibility for his statements. Our conversation quickly turned into a walk down memory lane, when I was a young musician in his church. He lamented the wayward youth pastor, wondering what he could have done to have prevented the tragedy of his divorce.

I walked away an hour later feeling nothing had been resolved, yet harboring no ill will towards the pastor. He just seemed like a lonely old man looking for attention. Neither of us knew where my secret would take me just a few months later.

– 2 –
Don't Call It Love

JANICE AND I were cut from the same musical cloth. We shared a love of the same obscure Southern Gospel band we were sure no one on the West Coast had heard of. This fact became the fodder of her husband's ridicule. I became close to Janice and her husband, Aaron. They and their children appeared to be the perfect family.

Aaron was a writer whose irreverent and witty sense of humor matched my own. If there was an inappropriate comment to be made at an inappropriate time, people often looked to us to see which one would make it first. We became such good friends that, for the first time in years, I shared my secret. I was shocked to learn he had a secret of his own.

"I'm gay, too," he told me. "I haven't told anyone else. Ever." Aaron was 12 years older than me. His confession instantly drew us closer. Though I had been attracted to him because of his personality, there was no chance of a relationship. He was married. They had kids. I was a minister. We were all Christians. My attraction needed to be squelched, I resolved.

If I knew nothing else, I knew that I loved Jesus. My life frequently felt out of control in spite of my constant prayer, Bible reading, church attendance, and fasting, but deep in my soul I knew I wanted to serve the Lord; I felt the calling on my life. In fact, it wasn't uncommon to have total strangers tell me there was something unique or special about me, and that God had plans for me. Many times those "words of prophecy" gave me the strength to continue fighting the internal war that raged inside. God was aware of my struggles and failures and yet he saw fit to send someone to remind me that He loved me. That's how I saw it.

I spent a lot of time with Aaron and Janice in and out of church. Together, Aaron and I wrote plays in which Janice would star. Her silky smooth and soulful voice was powerful. Aaron had a way with words that made the Gospel message relevant and relatable. It was a magical time in my ministry and I felt good about the work we were doing.

I was surprised when I got a call from Aaron's wife months later. "Aaron's gone," she sobbed on the other end of the phone. "He left a note saying it was over and that he doesn't want to be married anymore. I don't know where he is. I don't know what to do. Have you heard from him?"

I hadn't. My minister impulses kicked in and I knew I needed to help put this family back together. I had grown to love them, all of them. Eventually Aaron called and said he wanted to talk with me. We met at his job and drove to lunch.

"I don't love Janice," he told me. "I'm not sure I ever loved her. She is very controlling and she has a lot of secrets."

"But what about your kids?" I asked.

"Only one of them is mine. Her daughter is from a previous relationship," he confided. He went on to tell me about her teenage daughter's abortion and Janice's multiple marriages. And there was more. Aaron was attracted to me.

I wasn't completely shocked, but definitely caught off-guard. At the same time, I was aroused. "This isn't right," I said. "We're Christians." My brain was saying one thing while my heart screamed another. I wanted a relationship with Aaron. Increasingly, I felt drawn to him. Infatuation and love were synonymous for me, especially since I'd tried to avoid experiencing either. Over the course of the next few months I continued to meet with Aaron, simultaneously encouraging him to repair his marriage while allowing our own conversation to go down a sexual path.

I nurtured the thought of a relationship with him. I wondered what it would be like to be a couple. Dating boys in high school was out of the question, though I fantasized about many of the boys with whom I went to school. Aaron was the first man I'd ever been able to talk to about my feelings and have them reciprocated. He understood what it was like to have those feelings, too. He understood what it was like to have to hide them and always be on guard against someone finding out.

Our meeting places became more secluded: we spent time alone in his apartment and at dimly lit parks late at night. Eventually, I gave in. We kissed. My body melted under the emotional exhaustion of fighting off what felt like the inevitable. I *knew* I was in love. The mental conflict had resolved itself, if only for the moment. It felt right. The consequences were huge: his family and my job. In fact, my entire life had been planned around a career in ministry. All of that would change in an instant, but in his arms, I felt accepted. Normal. The anxiety lifted and I could feel emotions.

All of the energy and effort I'd put into building a ministry, nurturing a talent and creating a persona suddenly and instantaneously dissolved. I was loved and desirable. I didn't have to perform. I didn't have to hide my thoughts or sexual desires. I could just be me. The thought of having a life like this trumped anything I'd ever wanted.

The following day I went to see my pastor and I resigned from my position as the church's music minister. I had another part time job that kept money coming in while I tried to figure out what to do next. Amid tears, I confessed to my pastor what had been going on with my sexuality. I told him I was in love and, if it were possible, I would marry Aaron. I was ready to move forward, away from the mental and emotional conflict that had dominated my life. Ironically, it was only months after fighting for my Assemblies of God credentials.

The resolve to embrace my sexuality, however, was only a brief respite. The next weekend, Aaron and I headed to Disneyland with his kids, who knew nothing about our relationship. As we sat in the car, I was overcome with guilt. I wanted to cry, but didn't want to create a scene and bring up unwanted questions from his children. We made a pit stop at Aaron's parents' house, midway between Sacramento and L.A. His mom welcomed her grandchildren with open arms and soon began preparing dinner. I stepped outside for some air. Remorse engulfed me. Familiar anxiety gripped me.

"What's wrong?" Aaron asked.

"I can't do this," I said. "I don't want to be gay. This isn't right." We walked into an open field a few yards from his parents' house. The waft of fried chicken, which should have beckoned me back, filled the air. Instead, I felt nauseated. "I don't know how I'm going to get out of this, but I will," I told Aaron.

"You can't change," Aaron said. "We're gay and there's nothing we can do about it." We embraced as I dissolved into tears, overcome with guilt and shame. I couldn't bear to tell my parents what I was doing. They would be so ashamed of me. I was ashamed of me. Nothing had changed; I was still a failure. How could I give in to this fleshly temptation? Somehow, I made it through the weekend. I didn't want to be with Aaron. I just wanted to go home.

My pastor told me I was still welcome to attend the church, though I had been relieved of all my duties as the music minister. I avoided questions from the congregation by simply saying, "Oh, I just needed a break." The family that had become my second family, into which I put most of my time and energy, was gone. They had all left the church and I was alone again. I felt confused, and scared.

A Glimmer of Hope

I remembered, a couple of years earlier, seeing an episode of the Phil Donahue show on which he interviewed a man named Sy Rogers. Sy claimed to be a former transgender. He was articulate, intelligent and quick-witted. He effortlessly answered Donahue's questions and brushed off the host's doubts about his experiences. I listened intently and felt a wave of courage build up in my spirit.

I imagined myself, like Sy, talking to people on national TV about how God had delivered me from homosexuality and how he had the power to change people. It felt invigorating. I assumed that if it took Sy years to change back from a transgendered person to a male, I could easily change my sexual orientation. After all, I was already a Christian and did not see myself as gay. At the time I heard Sy, I didn't have any homosexual experiences to speak of. Now, that had changed. His message was more relevant than ever.

I opened the Yellow Pages and started to do some research. I discovered an organization in the San Francisco Bay Area called Love in Action that aimed to help Christians who struggled with homosexuality. I didn't know anything about them, but I knew I didn't want to get mixed up in a cult. Still, they seem to be the only organization around that offered any kind of hope. I began corresponding with someone named Mark.

Mark and I sent letters back and forth for several weeks. He explained how Love in Action had changed his life and what the ministry was doing for people just like me. I assumed the ministry was there for *real* homosexuals, who were degenerate and lost. He said there were others in the ministry who grew up in church and they, too, were able to bring their homosexuality to resolution.

On a Friday afternoon I jumped in my car and drove to San Rafael, California, to attend my first "ex-gay" Bible study. There I met Frank Worthen, who had founded the ministry, and his wife, Anita. The house where the Bible study was held was an older home just off the main highway. Frank, a wealthy former businessman, had added rooms and created the world's first live-in program for gay men. He offered explanations, from a Christian Evangelical perspective, on why homosexuality existed and how it could be overcome.

I have to admit that some of the people in the Bible study creeped me out, though I found the leaders, Frank and his wife in particular, to be warm and caring. I had talked with Anita on the phone previously. Following the Bible study, they invited me to talk with them in their studio apartment, which was located next to the house.

"God has more for your life," Anita said. "I know being gay feels normal, but it's not. It's the result of our sinful nature. Jesus can take away that pain and bring healing." She pointed to Frank, an unassuming man who'd felt the conviction to change his sexual orientation at the age of 43, as evidence of change.

From my evangelical perspective, everything they said made sense. I felt I was finally with people who were going through what I had been going through my entire life. They believed what I believed Biblically, including speaking in tongues and God's ability to heal people physically and emotionally. Nothing they said was scripturally inaccurate, as far as I was concerned. I cried, partly from the relief of being able to share my emotional conflict with people who understood, and partly because I felt I needed to move away from my family and into the live-in program. If ever I felt conviction from the Holy Spirit about my sin, and how to escape it, it was that night.

I drove back to Sacramento with a lot on my mind. I needed to tell my parents about everything. It was time to come out of the closet, as it were, about my struggle with same sex attraction. *At least*, I concluded, *I'm telling them with the prospect of becoming straight.*

I spent that week praying, reading my Bible and crying. I felt ashamed and hopeful. Finally, I called my pastor and told him I wanted to tell my parents what was going on. He agreed to meet with us at my parents' house and help me with the disclosure. My father was on the board at the time, but the pastor, put in an awkward position, had managed to keep my struggle private. When we arrived at my parents' house, I knew this would come as a shock to them.

We sat in their living room and my pastor nodded in deference to me so I could explain why we were there. "I, uh…" I couldn't say it out loud and looked at my pastor for help.

"Do you want me to tell them?" he asked. I nodded my head yes. Tears filled my eyes and I was so overcome with emotion I couldn't speak.

"Tim struggles with homosexuality and fell into sin," he said. "I've been working with him for quite some time to address his issues. He's repentant and has asked the Lord for forgiveness. He wanted to tell you what was going on, but this has been difficult for him."

"I found a place that helps people like me." I choked back the tears and the humiliation I felt.

My father, with steadfast assurance, looked at me and said, "I may not agree with everything you do, but I love you and I will always love you." I knew my father was sincere. Deep down, I always knew he loved me. The shame and embarrassment I felt, however, kept me from truly embracing his sentiments. We cried together. My pastor asked us to pray as a family, so we stood in my parents' living room, held hands and prayed for God's guidance.

Afterward, I went on to tell my parents more about the ex-gay ministry and my intention to go through the live-in program. Though they had reservations, not knowing about the ministry or the people behind it, they were supportive of my decision. I didn't offer any more information about my past or what I'd been feeling than I had to. My emotions were raw and I felt exposed. Perhaps I should have felt relieved, but I couldn't shake the embarrassment of talking about sexual deviancy with my parents or the sense that I'd disappointed them. Deep depression would soon set in.

I was invited to dinner to learn more about the ministry from the 1989 participants. Love in Action's residential program ran from January to December, so it was still several months before I would enter the program. We sat around a large table in a dated dining room with an enormous bowl of spaghetti and meatballs in front of us.

As the food was passed around, Frank invited me to ask anything I wanted to know about the men or the program. I am naturally an introvert, so to speak about any topic in an intimate setting with 12 people I didn't know was unnerving. Discussing my deepest darkest secret with strangers was simply not going to happen.

Marty, a Texan with a Southern drawl and a laugh big enough to make his home state proud, saw my apprehension. "Well, I'll start," he said. I laughed nervously. I struggled to pay attention, trying not to drop the bowl of spaghetti or make too much noise with my utensils.

"I was basically out of money, out of drugs and out of lovers. That's what brought me here!" he said with a bellowing howl. Frank quietly chuckled while barely moving his mouth. Two of Frank's endearing characteristics were his irreverent sense of humor and the fact that no matter what emotion he had, he hardly changed expressions.

Marty scared me a little. I had never run out of money, thanks to my parents, never done drugs and I was unclear what a "lover" was. I couldn't relate to Marty. At the same time, I found him likable.

While the rest of the participants cleared away the dishes, Marty, Frank, Anita and I stayed behind to talk. "People come from all over," Anita said, "and they are in different places in their walks with Christ." Anita told me a little of her own story.

"God calls us to give up everything and follow Him," she said lovingly. "Sin leads us down a certain path and before we know it, we end up someplace we never thought we would be," she continued.

"When I was single, I said I would only sleep with a man once I was married. As time went on and marriage didn't happen I said, 'I'll only sleep with a man when I'm engaged.' When that wasn't working for me I said, 'Well, then I'll only sleep with a man if I'm dating him.' Finally, I said, 'Alright, well, never two at once.'"

I couldn't help but laugh. Anita was candid about her own struggles. Like Frank, she had a quick and irreverent sense of humor. I felt a special bond to the Worthens and they frequently opened their home and hearts to me. Anita checked in on me from time to time before the program began. "We're praying for you," she'd let me know.

I slowly resumed my musical responsibilities of leading worship and playing for services in church over the next few months before leaving for San Rafael. With Aaron and his family gone, I began sharing my struggle with my close friends to prepare them for my departure.

"I knew it!" my friend told his wife, Rachel, after my confession. Josh and Rachel were my closest friends. Rachel and I began singing together when I was 18 and she was 15. Rachel was as naïve as I was about homosexuality. She never saw it coming. Their love and support helped ease the pain, but I felt like I'd failed them, and everyone else. With my secret out in the open, shame consumed me.

One Sunday morning, though I was scheduled to play for the morning service, I decided I couldn't do it. I grabbed a bottle of anxiety medication a psychiatrist had prescribed for me and I swallowed several pills. The warning label read: "May cause cardiac arrest if taking more than prescribed." That's what I was counting on. I lay down on my bed, hoping to die. After 30 minutes, I felt nothing. My body didn't seem to be reacting, though emotionally I felt numb. My mother, at church before the service started, became worried and began looking for me.

My apartment was within walking distance to the church and I decided if I was going to live, I might as well go and play. The Church had become so ingrained my life I couldn't see living any other way. If I was breathing, I was there. I always thought I'd die on stage preaching or singing the Gospel. Today was as good a day as any for that to happen.

"We were wondering where you were," members of the congregation said to me as I made my way through the back of the church and up to the piano. I felt like I was dreaming. I was done crying. My emotions were gone. Throughout the service I operated on autopilot. I'd been a musician for years. My body knew what to do. Following the service, I just went home to sleep off the effects of the medication.

A few days later, I found myself alone with my mom. She asked why I was so late to church that day. "I can't do this anymore," I told her, breaking down into tears. "I tried to commit suicide. I don't want to live anymore."

To my surprise, my mother was overcome with emotion. She had always been my rock, emotionally level, practical, and able to guide me into making the right decisions. She pulled me close and held on as we cried together. She knew. I think a mother always does. Her heart was as broken as mine. She had silently, and helplessly, watched my world fall apart, offering hugs and encouragement as best she could. I felt I needed to stand on my own, face my own fight and work things out. She knew I had reached the end and her heart was broken, too.

Like so many other times when I'd given up, something kept me going through the hopelessness, the pain and utter despair. It was still several weeks before I'd leave for the ministry and I needed to hold on and keep going. Music, as always, was the balm for all my wounds.

I met my friend Georgia at the church one night to practice for an upcoming trio she, my friend Rachel and I were performing. Georgia was at least 30 years my senior and acted 30 years older than that. She had sung Gospel music for years, gone through throat surgery and ended up with a raspy baritone sound that was as gentle and soothing as she was. Georgia held a special place in my heart, so I explained to her why I was leaving.

"It sounds painful," she said. It took me a minute to put the pieces of her response together. To my horror I suddenly realized that, to Georgia, homosexuality was synonymous with anal sex. I was mortified.

"Ewwww!" I responded. "How could you even think of that?!" My friend Rachel couldn't stop laughing. I knew Georgia had a heart of gold and her words were probably more for shock value than what she actually believed or thought. Still, I couldn't put anything past her. She usually said what she thought and fortunately, it was usually said with love and humor.

Georgia and many others expressed their love through hugs and letters during the interim before I left for Love in Action. I assumed it was because my confession was accompanied by a resolve to deal with it. I didn't think they would love me if I just threw in the towel and accepted being gay. Quite frankly, I wouldn't have been able to accept myself if I threw in the towel either. Accepting homosexuality was off the table. That would be the same as giving up. Besides, Christianity was my life and I knew it was incompatible with the Scriptures. I had to persevere.

In the weeks that followed I prayed more earnestly. I roamed the bedroom of my apartment reciting and memorizing entire books of the New Testament. I must have sounded like a mad man to the downstairs neighbors. I begged God to take away my homosexual thoughts and feelings. I asked for prayer during the altar calls, which was especially difficult for me, not wanting to be seen as weak or vulnerable. I certainly didn't want the attention. I'd think back to Sy Rogers on the Phil Donahue show and beg God for a miracle so I wouldn't have to go to the ex-gay ministry at all. I'd fantasize about telling people of the deliverance God brought me because I stayed faithful, prayed and studied the Word. Still, nothing changed.

My relationship with God grew cold. I followed Him out of sheer obedience, not because I wanted to. Besides, what else could I do? There was God or there was sin. Though I was frustrated with God, I had no choice but to submit to Him.

It was with a mixture of defeat, humiliation and anticipation that I left Sacramento for the ex-gay ministry. Like I'd done all my life, I still tried to fix myself single-handedly. Asking for help was putting myself in a vulnerable position. Honestly, I believed no one cared enough or loved me enough to really want to help. I certainly didn't want to bother anyone else with my problems.

Depression was now more like an old friend than a bothersome neighbor. I never thrived, but lived on the edge of what I considered success. I peaked musically, and learned to get by as a speaker, but kept myself from standing out or being different. Too much attention was threatening; not enough attention meant I wasn't worthy. I walked a dichotomous line of wanting to be validated and wanting to remain unnoticed. Without any fanfare I quietly ended my time at the church and silently disappeared into the next chapter of my life.

~ 3 ~
THE PROMISE OF CHANGE

IN JANUARY OF 1990, I entered the Love in Action program. It was New Year's Day that I, and my fellow participants, met each other at our assigned locations. Rick, who I learned was going to bunk with me, was from Alabama. He was outgoing, down-to-earth and easily made friends. Brent came from a small farm town in Nebraska, and though friendly, was a little awkward around the other guys. His grandfatherly demeanor, though he was only in his mid-twenties, made me feel safe around him. Nathaniel was a tall, good-looking artist. If I had a type, it would have been him with his kind blue eyes and blonde hair. Justin was a tall, awkward-looking guy from Wisconsin. Stephen was the youngest housemate at just 18 years old. He was, at the time, the live-in ministry's youngest participant. Stephen was outgoing with a defiant personality that would later lead to his demise. Travis was a married Methodist Minister and businessman. Love in Action was a last resort for him. He felt the full pressure to "get fixed" and save his marriage.

Our house leaders included Dave, who was HIV-positive, Randall, and Gerald. Marty, the Texan I'd met before I arrived also stayed with us. He was training to be an assistant house leader, but the ministry felt he had bigger issues to deal with before he was ready. Smoking was one of the things he needed to stop doing before he could be let loose to minister to the guys in the house. Frank had taken Marty under his wing. He wanted to help Marty continue to grow and, therefore, allowed him to stay with us.

I had no experience with people with AIDS or HIV. In 1990, the country was still reeling from the AIDS epidemic and misinformation abounded. I was mildly afraid of contracting AIDS during my stay, but Dave seemed perfectly healthy. I believed God had placed him in my life.

There was a second live-in house, where 12 more guys and their house leaders stayed. Our houses, though operating separately, interacted during Bible studies, church and group activities.

An immediate camaraderie developed among most of the group because of our shared circumstances. Gay wasn't a word we used to describe ourselves. In fact, it was still a foreign concept to me because it was a label with which I could not identify. As a Christian, I believed I could not be gay. Others felt the same way. The house, for us, was a place to belong. Even if we didn't share all of the same experiences, we shared enough to understand each other's struggles.

Never one to adapt well to change, it took a while for me to feel comfortable with my new housemates. The stories I heard from the other guys who had been more involved in the "homosexual lifestyle" were eye-opening. Some confessed to drug abuse, sexual escapades, alcoholism, and lives in the underbellies of their hometowns. Love in Action was their way out. Then there were those like me, who were simply there to deal with unwanted same-sex attraction.

Two weeks after we arrived at the ministry we were taken to a retreat center called "The Lord's Land" in Mendocino County,

California. The Lord's Land is a ranch that sits along the coast of Northern California. It offers a serene place of self-contemplation amidst trees and breaking ocean waves, with frigid to mild January temperatures. We stayed in an old farmhouse where beds lined multiple rooms on the second floor. During the winter months, a constant cold draft swept through the walls and floors of the house, which was heated only by a large wood stove on the first floor. Two bathrooms on the second floor served all of us. Not one for camping, I couldn't get my thin frame sufficiently warm.

The purpose of the retreat was to get to know each other and share our stories, or "testimonies" as they were called. One by one we were placed on the stairs in the old farmhouse and asked to share our painful stories of rejection, disconnection from God and sinful involvement with homosexuality. Many of the men told tragic stories of family dysfunction and being thrown out of their homes. Some confessed to sex and alcohol addictions, while others told how they contracted HIV. They talked about the sad consequences of poor decisions, which ultimately led to unhappiness and disillusionment inside the gay community.

Sometimes I wondered if I was in the right place. My story was a walk in the park compared to most of these guys. My parents never rejected me and most of my sexual experiences were with pornography. At the same time I wondered how these guys had managed to sink so low. Where were their inner voices telling them to stop? How could they claim to be Christians and end up in bars in the first place? I made no connection from my insulated and often narrowly focused brand of religion to theirs. Nor did I think back to my Bible school days when I so harshly judged my fellow preaching majors for their carnal deeds of defiance against God. I saw acting alone as more righteous than acting out with someone else. Still, there I was right with them in a rustic ranch house in the middle of nowhere. Soon it was my turn to tell my story and it occurred to me that I didn't have that much to say compared to everyone else.

I'd been in the ministry long enough to learn to speak in front of a crowd. In fact, Jimmy Swaggart was my television mentor. I admired his choice of words and the conviction with which he said them. Frantically, I thought of ways to make my story more dramatic. I knew I needed to cry at the end if I were to make a memorable impact. Though scared, I took my turn on that staircase.

I told the sad tale of my time with Aaron, how I'd never been attracted to girls and the familiar disconnection of the relationship with my father. Honestly, even I wasn't moved by the story. It lacked the excitement of the other guys' testimonies. I couldn't muster enough self-compassion to elicit sympathy from others. Even among these men, I didn't feel that I, or my story, measured up. Nevertheless, sharing our testimonies helped us learn more about each other. The vulnerability we shared made us feel closer. We were all in this together, committed to tackling the tough issues in our lives and becoming more like Christ.

Until I entered Love in Action, I'd never realized how sheltered I'd been growing up. Most of my life was spent in church and church was a place to experience intense emotions. I'd never been to a bar or taken drugs. I'd never gone dancing or been to a club. I'd never been drunk and barely tasted alcohol at all. I didn't know there was such a thing as anonymous sex and, even if I'd wanted it, I didn't know where to find it. I learned that some of these guys were able to find anonymous sex by simply making eye contact with men at a bookstore or a department store. I always looked away when people made eye contact with me.

We were taught that we were all the same: broken vessels of God who needed healing. I never felt comfortable with the idea that we were all the same. It was evident to me that the consequences of some of these people's actions put their minds in a different place. Perhaps it was guilt, perhaps they were psychologically unhealthy to begin with, but I could see in their eyes that they had experiences to which I couldn't relate and their issues were deeper than mine. I saw this recurring theme throughout my time in the ministry. The issues men and women brought to the ministry were sometimes much greater than we were qualified to address. The ministry lumped it all together as sin. It was a sweeping categorization to which only one remedy needed to be applied: repentance.

We were required to search for employment after we arrived back at the live-in house, following the retreat. I found an entry-level position at a mortgage company. It was just a few miles from the house and seemed to be the perfect job for where I was at the time. I quickly made friends at work, but gave evasive answers for why I was in the Bay Area.

At night, our house operated like a large family. We helped with dinner, chores, shopping and cleaning. We met nightly for Bible study, prayer groups and learning what caused us to be gay in the first place. We were encouraged to pray with each other away from the Bible studies and build godly relationships.

The first three months of the ministry were especially intense, as we were not allowed contact with the outside world, except for going to work. We could communicate with our families only through phone calls and letters. Whenever we left the house we were required to go in pairs or more. Whatever sexual feelings I might have had during this time simply disappeared. I was afraid of my own thoughts. When those feelings came back, I felt defeated. It was better to not have sexual feelings at all, I'd decided, than to have perverted ones.

Sexual attractions to one another did happen during the ministry. When they did, we were encouraged to talk with our house leaders about them. I found it helpful to discuss my attraction toward other participants, but it didn't alleviate the attraction. Forever the rule-follower, I did what I was told and chalked up the attraction to my sin and sickness. I was obedient and pushed the thoughts out of my head and suppressed my feelings. I learned to do that well.

Frank led Bible studies and had created a workbook based on his book, *Steps Out of Homosexuality* (1984). We were taught that our homosexuality was caused by a broken relationship with our fathers. Many times, Frank said, sexual molestation was also a cause of homosexuality. He encouraged us to pray and think about experiences that might have led us to where we were. Nonetheless, psychologically we had been separated from our God-given sexual identities and that allowed the devil to come in and put doubts in our minds about who we were meant to be. In our rebellion, we pursued sexual relationships with members of the same sex.

I always felt disconnected from my father, so Frank's words made sense. At one point Frank asked us to write letters to anyone in our lives whose influence had possibly led us down the wrong path and whom we needed to forgive. I knew my father loved me, but his words were, at times, abusive. In my letter I wrote:

...what I remember most about my childhood is a lot of fear. I was always so frightened of when my dad was going to come home. I didn't know what kind of mood he would be in. I didn't know if he would be glad to see me or if I was only going to get in his way. I tried to be smart for him. I tried to help him...I wanted so desperately to find rest in the gentle strength of his arms and feel the peace from his soothing voice of comfort. I never found that...I always tried to be normal. I thought I was expected to get married at 22 and be emotionally stable and have a family. It's what I wanted and it's what I thought my father would want. But once again, I failed...

And my father wrote back:

Even though our relationship was strained...I have and always will love you, and I wished I could have brought myself to express my feelings...I thought the way to show that you are the head of your house was to be stern and always tell your wife and children their faults, [but it] was a sign of weakness. You see, I grew up around my father who at no time while I was growing up ever said he loved me, or that he was proud of me. So, I too did not say I was sorry...I desire that closeness, that you will not ever fear you can't confide in me. As I grow in the Lord I pray that my past will become a memory, and my future a godly hope. Son, please remember even when I can't show my emotions, I love you with all that is within me.

The relationship I have with my father today is thanks in large part to my time at Love in Action. The ministry was the catalyst for learning to accept him as a human being and relate to him as an adult.

In many ways I learned to be a man at Love in Action. I was always independent and self-sufficient, but I learned how to let my guard down, show some of my emotions, and develop healthy relationships with both sexes. "You're only as sick as your secrets" was an overly used but true mantra of the ministry. I took responsibility for my feelings and actions, which I found in itself to be empowering.

I met Sy Rogers, the man from the Phil Donahue show, who inspired me to seek help for change. He was a friend of the Worthens and came to our house for a visit. I'd never met anyone from TV before and I was truly star-struck. Sy was as personable, charismatic and funny in person as he had been on the show.

Frank called the guys together so we could meet Sy and ask him questions. I simply stared at him and hung on his every word. Someone brought up the Phil Donahue show and I blurted out, "I loved how you put him in his place." Sy never tried to put people in their places. He simply spoke the truth, as he saw it. I felt embarrassed by my comment. Sy graciously smiled and moved on.

Sy's association with the ministry made me feel like I was part of something much bigger than myself. I knew Frank and Anita had made appearances on a number of popular Christian television shows and, occasionally, they would casually drop the name of a Christian celebrity they knew. They seem to be on the cusp of big work that God was doing in the gay community and I felt I was in the right place.

Love in Action was also part of a church that we were required to attend. It was a small family church that believed the basic tenets of the Evangelical Pentecostal faith, including prophecies and speaking in tongues, as well as the virgin birth, death and resurrection of Christ. The pastors were oddly non-charismatic personalities. In fact, they rubbed me the wrong way. I couldn't get used to congregational prayer, which was mostly silent, non-inspirational worship led by a guitar player, and the conglomeration of eccentrics in the congregation. I was certainly used to strange people. It seemed Pentecostalism drew the oddest personalities into our congregations. But this place was very different from the church in which I was raised.

As a child I fell asleep in the pew to noise. Our pastors were fire-and-brimstone screamers with charismatic personalities and booming voices that preached inspirational sermons. Up until Bible College this was all I had ever known. Yet, even in college I managed to find a non-denominational church that mimicked my cultural experiences. Churches that prayed quietly and played somber music were more reminiscent of going to a library than to a church. Experiencing this new culture was as much of a disruption in my way of thinking as attending Frank's classes.

The men weren't allowed to be involved in any type of ministry during the first several months of the program. Love in Action believed there should be a time of healing and we shouldn't be in the limelight or have any ministry pressures on us. I appreciated the fact that they wanted to get to know me for me, but my talent was an extension of my relationship with God. I felt like I was being asked to have that relationship without using my voice.

We attended weekly Bible studies at church members' homes. That allowed us to get more involved with the members of the church and create personal relationships. Everyone was loving and accepting. They were all aware of Love in Action's presence. In fact, many members of the congregation were alumni of the ministry who chose to stay in the area and in the church following their time in the program. No one judged us for being gay, or ex-gay, or for participating in the program. Many admired our commitment to change.

There were others in the program who also struggled to find their places. Nathaniel, the artist, had begun an already successful career in television. Leadership told him that he needed to surrender his gifts to God. In a show of obedience Nathaniel took some of his art and tools and buried them in the sand near an ocean shore. He was "crucifying" himself and giving up his very being to follow God. He struggled to work a nine-to-five job. It wasn't who he was. Resentment quietly built and his beliefs were shaken. I, like the leadership, felt it was necessary for a season, but watched Nathaniel grapple with his faith.

Our house was riddled with untapped talent: actors, singers, songwriters, and artists. Sadly, the prevailing thought was that these talents did not glorify God if they were not used in the Church. People were asked to give up parts of their personalities if the ministry identified those things as related to their homosexuality. In contrast, everything I'd ever done was for the ministry and I had no connection to the secular world. The guys would sometimes bring up pop or dance tunes they heard in the bars. I didn't listen to secular music. I was frequently an outsider to those conversations.

I struggled with my friendships with many of the men in the house. It took me a long time to let my guard down and feel like I was part of a group. Though I made great strides to blend in, I never felt completely comfortable in the environment. By March of 1990, I had settled into a routine and was allowed to have visitors from Sacramento.

"So this is it, huh?" Rachel said. We sat in the living room, just adjacent to the front door. I introduced Rachel and her husband to some of the guys as they walked by. It was an unusually relaxed day at the Love in Action live-in house.

"So how's the music going at church?" I asked. I looked for ways to make small talk and avoid the embarrassment I felt about where I was. If I had been a successful Christian, I subconsciously reasoned, we wouldn't be sitting here having an awkward conversation in someone else's house.

"It's fine," Rachel said. She had grown up as sheltered in the Church as I was, so I knew she was still confused by what I was doing and how it all worked. She loved me anyway, though I was never really able to accept it.

We left the house and had lunch at a restaurant a few miles down the road before Josh and Rachel went back home. I had been happy to have a piece of familiarity with me, if only for a couple of hours, but blending my worlds together wasn't comfortable.

As summer approached my anxiety began to subside and I felt more content in my surroundings. We went, as a program, on several outings, which included trips to Sacramento to tour the state capital, Frank's home in Aptos for a weekend beachside vacation, trips to the beach, a group tour of San Francisco, and hikes through the famed Muir Woods Redwood Forest in Mill Valley, California.

One night Marty and I went with a couple of the other guys to see a movie. The movie contained a love scene that, though not explicit, triggered a deep emotion in me. Out of the blue, I broke down crying.

"Whoa, there Tim. You alright?" Marty put his hand on my back.

"I don't know," I said. Even I was unclear about why I had such a strong reaction. I'd had flashbacks of my time with Aaron. Now, I wasn't even sure how to identify what I felt about him. I'd thought I loved him, but I had no experience with being in love. Over the past few months, the ministry taught me that gay love was really not love at all, just sinful feelings. I didn't want that. In fact, I wanted to be as far away from those feelings as possible. I was frustrated by my own reaction to something as simple as two people showing affection on a movie screen.

Ironically, not long after that experience, I received a letter from Aaron. I hadn't heard from him since he left the church. "Tim, I wanted you to hear it from me. I've met a lady named Vicki and we're getting married."

I didn't know what to make of the letter. He left his first wife because he was gay, told me he couldn't change and then jumped right back in the closet? How could he do that? Why couldn't I do that? Why did this thing eat at my soul? *It won't last*, I told myself. Whatever subliminal hope I was still holding onto for our relationship, if any at all at this point, was most definitely gone. I imagine it's like finding out in your late forties you cannot have children. Even if you never wanted them, there's something about losing the option that messes with your head.

Aaron's letter confirmed that whatever it was between us was nothing more than a sexual experience. The feelings I felt were all lies. None of it was real. It was evidence that God had snatched me out of the depths of sin and put me back on a path of righteousness. That's what I told myself, though I don't know that I believed it.

The conflicts and resolutions in our house drew us together. We learned to accept others as they were with the caveat that we were there to help draw each other closer to God and further from our sin. There were no major dramas that happened during that year, at least in our house. The other live-in house, on the other hand, seemed to be fraught with drama and disobedience. The devil, it appeared, spent all his time over there and left us alone. Our house concluded the year among Love in Action's success stories.

1990 was an intense year of emotional healing for me. For the first time in my life I felt like one person. My secret was finally out and dealt with, as far as I was concerned. I identified myself as an ex-gay man. People in the ministry understood me and understood all that ex-gay stood for: someone who had turned his back on sin and been delivered from homosexuality through Christ. I knew that God loved me and wanted the best for me. I even began to fantasize that one day I would be married.

As the year grew to a close I reflected on the changes that had taken place. Pornography was no longer part of my life and it felt good to be free of the guilt that accompanied it. Fantasizing about male relationships certainly hadn't gone away, but I believed one day that it would. I felt more in control of my thoughts as I practiced taking every thought captive "to make it obedient to Christ" (1 Corinthians 10:5). My parents and I had become much closer. I began to see them as human beings and looked forward to the time we spent together.

I felt my thoughts, actions and feelings were more in line with what I believed, and my future finally began to look promising after all those years of struggle. Leaving the live-in program was like having my braces removed. How well I would do without them depended on whether or not I would wear my "ex-gay retainer."

– 4 –
MY EX-GAY LIFE

AT THE END of 1990 I decided to stay in the Bay Area. I moved into an apartment in the neighboring city of Novato. My roommate, Ken, was a house leader for Love in Action's other house during my program year. Ken also worked as the event coordinator for Exodus International. Love in Action and Exodus International shared office space in San Rafael. Rick, my roommate from the live-in program, moved in with us. The three of us eventually became close friends, hanging out, praying together and sharing our struggles. Whenever one of us felt attracted to someone of the same gender, we talked about it and asked what we thought was triggering the temptation. As we had been taught, we usually recited our own insecurities as men. The person to whom we were attracted had what we felt we lacked: confidence, looks, personality, etc. Our conversations were deep, heartfelt and filled with brotherly concern. I had never experienced friendships on such a level before.

Rick, however, seemed to struggle with staying out of trouble. On several occasions he confessed his temptation and sexual activities. I grew increasingly frustrated with him. "You say you don't want to do this," I reprimanded him, "but you never call us *before* an incident, you only tell us *afterward*." Looking back I realize now that I was still more concerned with the appearance of keeping it together than dealing with reality. Rick was always real and honest. If he had a fall, he talked about it. If he had an impure thought, he said it. If he felt something, he didn't think twice about stating it. I, on the other hand, needed to keep up the appearance that I was living a pure life. For all practical purposes I was staying out of trouble, but the energy and effort I put into maintaining that appearance would eventually lead me down a familiar path.

In the mean time, I felt I had sufficiently conquered same-sex attraction and was focused on finding the woman of my dreams. I knew I would never feel the same way towards women as I felt for men. The ministry explained this by saying, "God does not replace one sin with another" and that the sexual attraction would reveal itself when I found the right woman. In some ways, it was explained to me, ex-gay men were better off than straight men. We had to deal with our unnatural desires and that gave us the ability to better cope with sexual temptation. All sexual temptation was sinful lust unless it was within the confines of marriage, we believed. It had to be controlled, conquered and brought into the submission of Christ. I'd grown accustomed to looking away or changing my focus when I saw an attractive man. I believed I could maintain this for the rest of my life with God's help.

BACK IN THE MINISTRY

Around June of 1991, I was getting anxious to get back into the ministry. I'd been working at my job in the mortgage company for a year and a half and I was getting bored. My heart was, and had always been, in preaching the Gospel. Love in Action was the perfect place for me to do that, especially with my newfound freedom.

Frank and Anita felt the calling to start a new ministry in the Philippines and relinquished their leadership of Love in Action to John Smid. John, who we affectionately called Smiddy, began working with the ministry in 1987 as a house leader and Frank had groomed him to take over. John tells his story in his book: *Ex'd Out: How I Fired the Shame Committee* (2012).

At this time the media attention around gay rights and the ex-gay message was heating up. Love in Action received an enormous amount of exposure and frequently received requests for speaking engagements, interviews, and television shows. Sensing an opportunity, I approached Smiddy to ask if I could lead the outreach program for the ministry.

"You're not going to believe this," John said, "but the board and I just had a discussion about this very thing last night. We need someone to handle all of the requests we're getting." It was a marriage made in heaven, as far as we were concerned. I became the ministry's new Outreach Director.

I worked as a volunteer for several months. After work I'd go into the office and take phone calls or call people back to set up interviews and manage the calendar. When Frank was directing the ministry he frequently took the men and women from the live-in programs and Bible studies to churches to do what he called "rallies." These rallies included worship, testimonies and plays. I revamped his rally idea and changed the name to "outreaches."

I pulled together the talent I recognized in many of the alumni who stayed in the area following their time in the ministry, as well as some of the top-notch performers I had worked with through the years in Sacramento. I coordinated speakers, organized the program, led worship and sang new songs I'd written. The band sounded professional and our program was inspiring. The demand for sharing our ministry grew. We traveled throughout Northern California and held an annual outreach in Marin County at a large local church, where we advertised and invited others in the Christian community to hear our message of freedom and change.

I was back in the ministry with a renewed vision and a new energy. I also had the opportunity to work with some big name television shows getting our staff and leaders on TV. We were interviewed by Good Morning America, Dr. James Kennedy's Coral Ridge Ministries, and the 700 Club, among others.

RELIGION AND POLITICS
Unintentionally, Love in Action's message became the heart of the moral and political debate over homosexuality and reparative therapy. In 1992, Focus on the Family approached the ministry to participate in a new video called "The Gay Agenda." We had no idea who else was appearing in the video, nor did we know the title at the time. John Paulk and John Smid were interviewed from our ministry, both offering firsthand accounts of some of the more solicitous highlights of sexual behavior by some members of the gay community. We didn't see our involvement as political, but merely sharing the depravity to which sin can lead people without God.[1]

John Paulk was one of the Love in Action staff members who had served as a house leader at the other house during my year in the program. He was a 1988 alumnus of the ministry and Frank Worthen also took John under his wing. Frank, like so many of us, saw something special and different in John Paulk. To distinguish him from John

Smid, we called him JT for John Tom. A previous program member had nicknamed him and it stuck.

JT's story was as unique as he was. He was a convincing former female impersonator in a small Ohio town and seemed destined for the spotlight. Naturally articulate, a gifted singer, and creatively inspired, JT stood out. With pictures from his drag days he offered a visually, as well as verbally, dramatic story of change. He inspired thousands, traveling around the

---

[1] As a side note, only recently did I discover how far reaching our involvement with the Christian right had gone. The Gay Agenda video, I learned, was used to deny LGBT rights in the state of Oregon through a 1992 ballot Measure 9. Twenty-two years later, in 2014, armed with the same information, the Center for Arizona policy pushed Senate Bill 1062, which allowed discrimination to the LGBT community based on religious beliefs. The Center for Arizona Policy is led by Cathi Herrod (Sanchez and Marquez, 2014), who was a longtime friend and supporter of Love in Action. We spoke for Cathi and her group at the time, Concerned Women for America, in venues in Phoenix and Tuscon during the early '90s, providing them plenty of ammunition. The rhetoric we used– people are gay because of poor parental relationships, molestation and broken homes – is used the same way today by these organizations.

Sanchez, Ray, Marquez, Miguel, February 21, 2014, CNN.com, Arizona Lawmakers Pass Controversial Anti-gay Bill, http://www.cnn.com/2014/02/21/us/arizona-anti-gay-bill/, retrieved March 7, 2014

country with Love in Action. Soon, JT was pulled into the television circuit. Everyone wanted to hear about his transformation.

I often felt eclipsed by JT and his story. We had heard it so many times it became fodder for teasing him in the office. His drag pictures inspired the "hall of shame" where we took headshots of other members of the Love in Action and Exodus International staff, made them look like the opposite sex and posted the pictures on the back of an inside office door. It was all in fun and helped alleviate some of the midday boredom.

We could nearly recite each other's testimonies word for word. My story didn't include all of the twists, turns and pictures JT's story did. I pitied his past substance abuse and his involvement in the gay lifestyle, to which I couldn't relate, and even some of the family experiences he had. Yet, I was jealous of his notoriety and his ability to always be who he was and live in the moment. I had spent so many years honing my "good Christian boy" image that I believed it myself. I wasn't aware of the shame that lurked beneath. I admired JT's shamelessness. Again, I felt the dichotomous pull to stand out and blend in. I wished I had a story like JT's, but it's not necessarily what I wanted to be known for.

JT eventually developed a relationship with Anne, a former lesbian in the ministry, and following their engagement, the two together became a national phenomenon. The Christian right pointed to them as God's proven power to change a person's sexual orientation, while the rest of the world was just confused. We were all stunned when Oprah Winfrey called and said she wanted to interview them. *We've hit the big time*, I thought. Oprah sent her team of cameramen to our office in preparation for the segment. We were asked to reenact a typical Bible study scenario for them to record for the show. To retain the anonymity of those in the program, our Bible study was made up mostly of staff members and a couple of volunteers. Never one for role-play, I remember someone making fun of me for how I stared at Smiddy, our mock Bible study leader, during the taping. My eyes glazed over. I tried to look interested, hearing him give the same spiel about why people are gay. By now, those words were ingrained in my memory.

Prior to the airing of the show I went through mental acrobatics trying to figure out who might see me on the Oprah show during that segment. I talked to my parents about telling the grandparents, but we decided that the chances they would see the show were probably slim. As it turned out, that segment never aired.

I constantly struggled with telling my story and talking about the ministry in the media while trying to keep my private life private. I didn't feel the stinging grip of shame from hiding my sexual identity; I was now trying to hide my very job from people I didn't know. I traded one shame for another.

JT and Anne went on to get married and I had the privilege of playing a song for them at their wedding. The ceremony was beautiful, down to the last detail. I remember feeling like I was a part of something much bigger than us. Our stories felt authentic and we believed our lives and messages were the very heart of God. JT and Anne's wedding confirmed that change truly was possible. Their world, as mine, was open to endless possibilities simply because we allowed God to take control of our lives and surrendered to His greater good.

Bob Davies, Exodus International's Executive Director at the time, was in the office next to ours. Bob had become a popular writer and author on the ex-gay movement. He had a quiet and humble demeanor. I'd gotten to know Bob through our church, where he played the piano on the worship team, and by working with him at the office. I began submitting articles for Love in Action's newsletter, which Bob also edited. He nurtured me as a fledgling writer.

"You have a unique way of writing and you're especially good at humor," he told me. I was honored that he even noticed. I'd never met an author before and I'd always loved writing. Bob taught me to how to edit the testimonies we received for the monthly newsletters. He told me how to submit articles for publications in magazines. Eventually, I would take over as the main editor for Love in Action's International Newsletter.

Our outreach ministry continued to expand with appearances on the Jerry Springer Show, Sally Jesse Raphael, and World News Tonight with Peter Jennings. I focused on speaking in colleges, universities and churches sharing my "church testimony" of growing up gay, and overcoming through prayer, Scripture and accountability. Ultimately, I appeared on over 30 radio and television shows, sang in churches across America and took nearly every opportunity to share our message. The travel was exciting, going from one town to the next and landing in one airport after another. I loved life on the road and I met a lot of interesting people.

Shawn introduced himself as I stepped off the stage at a Christian University somewhere in Ohio. "I always thought I was gay, but couldn't really meet anyone where I'm from," he explained with a soft, polite Midwestern drawl. He looked around nervously, hoping no one was paying attention to our conversation. His voice grew quieter.

"I…I…experimented with farm animals," he leaned forward to tell me.

I'd been to Bible school, taken classes in pastoral counseling, studied the Scriptures from every angle, and spent countless hours helping people over the phone, but I was not prepared for that confession. The only thought I had was, *Well, crap. If they covered this in class I must have missed that day.* To this day, I hope my outward expression didn't match the inward one.

"I don't really know where to go for help," Shawn continued

"Do you know of any ex-gay ministries around here?" I asked. I knew he didn't, but I needed to get him back to a topic I understood.

"No, and I don't think I can talk about it with any of my friends or classmates."

I offered to pray with Shawn and asked him to call the office. I told him we would look for someone he could connect with. I felt bad, knowing how difficult it was to be alone, but was at a complete loss for what to say. I assumed his acting out resulted from a lack of people; at least that's what I hoped.

We met a lot of people like Shawn, looking lost, troubled and hurting. In fact, we'd often climb back in the van on the way back to hotels or the airport and say things like, "Did anyone else notice the guy on the right side of the stage? He looked like he needed to talk." John Smid especially had a heart for people he'd see at our events. He'd often try to speak with them if he was able. They all made his prayer list.

In December, 1993 my first article, "Is it OK to be Gay?" was published in the Assemblies of God youth magazine, *On Course*. Rush Limbaugh graced the cover and I was proud to be associated with his politics and grass roots morality, though I didn't see the bigger political connection. Rush was also from Sacramento, so I was familiar with his show. I had even walked by his house because he lived near a friend.

I didn't dwell too much on the conflict between the gay community, politics and its connection to the Church. I felt what we were doing was right, but gay people didn't know it yet. I often quoted the

Scripture that said we were the salt and light of the earth (Matthew 5:13) and presumed that it meant we had an obligation to preserve the morality in the world and show people the right way to live. Love in Action's message was widely accepted in Evangelical Churches, and in the post-Reagan era, American society was generally morally conservative. Other than liberal areas, like the Bay Area where we operated, our message was popular. It offered an explanation for homosexuality that even the un-churched could accept.

Working with other ex-gay leaders, we developed a method for reaching youth who struggled with same sex attraction. It was a no-nonsense approach to confused youth that explained how to align their sexual orientation with God's pure intent. We presented our message in public schools and to church leaders. A co-presenter and I gave one of the first messages on the topic of youth and homosexuality at the San Diego Exodus International Conference in 1995. The video, as well as my published article, would later haunt me as I struggled to distance myself.

Later, a radio station in Santa Rosa, California, invited me to speak on its popular morning talk show. It sounded like a great opportunity to propagate our message of hope and change, so I took this particular engagement thinking it was just going to be the host and me. I was naïve enough to think back then that an invitation to speak implied agreement with our message. I was about to find out neither of those things were true. The show included two activist, angry lesbians, the combative host, and mild-mannered me.

The DJ's introduction went something like this: "Ladies and gentlemen, it's a pleasure to have in the studio this morning with me, Dawn and Liz, two dear ladies who are active members of the LGBT community. And on the phone is Tim from Love in Action who thinks he can change people from gay to straight." I never even got the chance to say hello. It was clear from the outset that this was going to be the longest hour of my life.

I did what I had learned to do when dealing with the media. I gave them sound bites and made sure I hit my three main points: Jesus Christ is Lord, He loves you, and there is freedom from homosexuality through Jesus Christ. I was unbending in my message, confident and sure. But the women and I hit an impasse when one of them asked, "If a gay couple came into your church, would you welcome them?"

"Yes, absolutely," I said.

"So you accept gay people," she said.

"We accept people as they are and allow God to change them as he changes all of us," I assured her.

"So you don't accept gay people as they are," she responded.

"No, we do, but God loves them too much to leave them that way," I said. This made the ladies angry, or maybe I should say angrier.

"You know what?" the other woman said, "What are you going to do 20 years from now when you come to realize you are gay, nothing's changed and you have no place to go?!"

It was never a thought that entered my mind before, or even years after that encounter. I was right and she was wrong.

I told myself that the most important thing was that we got the message out. Even if the interview went poorly, at least I could be certain there were people out there who heard it. I'd planted a seed of hope in them and they knew there was another option. My job was to spread the good news of the Gospel. I was prepared, somewhat, for opposition. After all, if they crucified Jesus for his message they would most certainly want to crucify me for mine.

Hope or Condemnation?

Our ministry was scheduled to teach a full day's seminar on freedom from homosexuality, sponsored by a local church. For whatever reason, the person slated to teach a class about pro-gay theology had to cancel and I was handed his notes. I had a simple understanding of the topic, but wasn't exactly comfortable picking up the class at the last minute. Never one to shy away from a challenge, I stood in front of a packed classroom. I tried to maintain eye contact, while keeping a close eye on the notes in front of me. My confidence grew as I watched people nod in agreement. Calling on my Bible school and ministry experience I spoke with authority.

"Clearly," I said with conviction, "God states that a man should not lie with a man as with a woman and there is no other way to interpret the Scriptures. So the idea that David and Jonathan were 'lovers' would have been an abomination and they would have been stoned to death." The audience agreed with me. Hands shot up during the question and discussion time where we shared Scriptures, doctrine and interpretation. The atmosphere was electrified. Our unanimous perspective on the topic confirmed that we were taking the right stand.

Finally, an elderly man sitting near the back of the class raised his hand. I'd noticed him earlier. He was dressed in a priest's collar, and stayed quiet throughout the rigorous discussion. His arms and legs had been folded. I assumed he was shy but expected that, like the rest of the participants, he stood with us in our views of the topics discussed.

"Yes?" I said pointing to the man.

"I came here today to find out what you had to say, but I didn't think you were going to attack my church." I stood speechless for a moment. Our ranks had been infiltrated by the enemy. I didn't expect that. Also, I had a sinking feeling that he had studied theology more than I had. He probably knew more than me, or at least he *thought* he did.

"I'm the pastor of the local MCC and I wanted to know what you had to say about the issue." He continued. "Nothing you have said is accurate. Quite frankly, it's offensive, homophobic and perpetuates exclusion of people in the gay community from the Church."

The MCC, or Metropolitan Community Church, is a world-renowned pro-gay church. It's what we considered apostate. As an evangelical, I believed they preached doctrine that told people what their "itching ears" wanted to hear, as described in 2 Timothy 4:3, and approved of immoral lifestyles.

While I was still trying to get my bearings, people in the crowd launched theological missiles and, in no uncertain terms, told him to be quiet. He was outnumbered with no place to go. He could only withdraw and retreat. I was appreciative of the response because I honestly had none. I was saved from the embarrassment of losing a battle of wits, but also felt he was unfairly treated. I quickly dismissed the thought that there was no fair discussion on the topic in favor of proliferating our *true* message of change and deliverance. I had done my job and, by almost all accounts, I had done it well.

During a break in the schedule I stepped outside and awkwardly ran into that pastor, who stood smoking on a secluded sidewalk. He nodded his head in acknowledgement of me. He seemed unhappy and lost, though perhaps he was merely lost in thought.

"How are you doing?" I said. I didn't really want to know; it was just my usual greeting. I could tell his defenses were down by the way he stood. Mine were up and I immediately looked for a graceful way to leave. It was just us on the walkway.

"You know, I was once involved in regular churches," he said, "but when it came out that I was gay, I wasn't welcomed anymore. I still believed in God. That didn't change. There are a lot of gay people who still believe in God."

I was as lost for words outside the classroom as I had been inside. "I'm sorry for what happened in there," I said. "They kind of ganged up on you and I felt bad about that." I couldn't think of a response to what he just said. His theology was wrong. That was the bottom line. I couldn't explain why he chose to be gay, but he was obviously making a choice contrary to the Word of God and then twisting the Bible to fit his lifestyle. God would never let someone like that into Heaven.

I turned and went back inside to talk to someone from the ministry who could make me feel better about my reaction to this guy. Before long, I pushed the whole experience out of my mind and chalked it up to another day of fighting the enemy and ministering to the people.

Just the "Facts"

I had already studied what little research there was on what made people gay, but mostly from the Christian perspective. After that class, I also studied gay theology to learn how to better speak to the issues and combat those who were deceptively misled into believing something other than the Bible, as it was meant to be interpreted. Always analytical, I tried to get more than one side of the issue. Even at that time, I felt much of what came from the Family Research Council, the research institute from Focus on the Family, didn't sit right. When they put out an article stating the average life span of a gay man was 44 years old, a seed of doubt was planted in my mind about the legitimacy of their study.

Jerry Falwell, Pat Robertson, and much of the Christian Right were focused on distributing information about the gay agenda. Most of what they had to say made sense to me as an evangelical. Gay people *did* seem to want more than equal rights; they wanted more rights than the general population at the expense of the rest of us. I also wondered what would happen if they got what they wanted. Where would it end? Like much of the Christian population, my only conclusion was outright moral chaos, with men marrying chickens and goats, and orgies in the street. I didn't feel a calling into the political realm, but I stayed the task and presumed that if I simply preached the Gospel, as I was called to do, I was making a difference.

Homosexuality, as I understood it from the ministry's perspective, was nothing more than rebellious debauchery. Homosexuals could never achieve the intimacy heterosexuals could because it wasn't God's design. The gay lifestyle was the devil's counterfeit for what God originally intended for the human race. I had come to believe that my attractions for members of the same sex were purely sexual in nature. No intimacy or good would have ever come from them. I was frequently thankful that God kept me from the degenerative lifestyle I had heard about from the other men in the program. Had I participated in that lifestyle it would have certainly led me into contracting AIDS and then to my death. Such a dramatic, predetermined conclusion both emphasized the grace God had extended to me and spiced up an otherwise mediocre testimony.

The ministry gave me significant satisfaction with where I was in life, but I longed for a heterosexual relationship. I watched JT and Anne's relationship flourish and I prayed for the same experience. I didn't necessarily feel attracted to women, but I believed what I had been taught: that it would all fall into place when the right one came into my life.

The Girl

I felt like I was on the top of my game in 1994 when I met the woman who would later become my wife. She was a very attractive 22-year-old, temporarily staying with my parents when we met. Our families attended the same church, where I had also been the music minister. She was six years younger than me and in the youth group at the time I was there. Though she was too young to know what I was going through back then, she was now aware of my past with same sex attraction. Like many in my home church, she admired my righteous struggle and the freedom I appeared to have found.

"You're going to marry her," my dad told me on a visit home.

I'm sure his proclamation was intended to push me toward her. Instead, I dug my heels in and said, "Well, God will have to tell me that Himself." Still, she and I became the best of friends over time and I entertained the thought of asking her out. Our conversations lasted for hours and we enjoyed each other's company.

Growing impatient, she was the first one to make the move and asked *me* out on Valentine's Day in 1994, our first official date. Naturally, I didn't feel an overwhelming sexual attraction toward her, but I was smitten with her. It was the idea of "normalcy" that

I was attracted to. I was certainly in love with the idea of being in love. Having a beautiful woman on my arm solidified my healing, if not to others, certainly to me.

She and I began alternating visits to each other's places every other weekend, when I was not gone traveling with the ministry. She lived in Sacramento and I was in the Bay Area, roughly 100 miles away. Whenever she was able, she attended my talks to youth groups and went with me to churches where I was speaking, or when the ministry held an outreach. Occasionally, she'd sit with me in the front of a youth group and answer questions about our relationship. Unlike relationships I'd had in the past, this one felt more natural. It wasn't accompanied by the intense anxiety that usually led to the demise of my relationships with the opposite sex.

Still, sexual attraction felt forced. I remember having a conversation with Anita Worthen, when they were in town one day and expressed my concern.

"Don't worry about it," she assured me. "If she's the right one then everything will work the way it is supposed to, when it's time. God knows what He's doing."

I trusted Anita. After all, she and Frank had been married for years and they seemed very happy. Frank and Anita, by their very existence, held out a silent hope for many of us. Frank frequently spoke about his relationship with Anita, including their sexual experiences. He told us how they navigated through their sex life and how God worked it out because He put them together.

I continued praying for direction over my relationship with my new girlfriend and sought advice from friends and family. I soon made the decision to ask her to marry me. Everyone agreed that our relationship was ordained by God, except for a couple of unrelated and unlikely people.

Smiddy, with whom I'd grown close, pulled me aside and said, "I have concerns about this girl. It seems like things are moving really fast and I don't think she's right for you."

Taken aback, I said, "Well, I think that's for me to decide." I didn't feel he knew her well enough to make a statement about her or our relationship. I felt he was overstepping his bounds by asking me to break off the relationship without any solid reasoning. Also, co-workers in the ministry had complained about how Smiddy had gotten too involved in their lives and said things he didn't earn the right to say. They felt he was trying to control them, they said. I discounted his words and ignored his advice.

In one other incident, my girlfriend, now fiancée and I went to visit our former pastor and his wife, Janine. When my fiancée had stepped away to use the restroom Janine asked me, "Are you sure you want to do this?" Normally, easy-going she turned suddenly serious and made direct eye contact.

"Yes, Janine," I said with certainty. "I've prayed about this and we've spent a lot of time together. I love her and I think this is the right thing to do." I giggled to relieve some of the tension. "Why are asking?"

"That family is *really* messed up. I mean *really*. I don't think you know what you're getting into." Her tone was serious.

I appreciated her concern because I knew she loved me, but at that point I'd been committed and I felt like God had orchestrated this marriage. My parents, whom I trusted, adored her. Everything was lining up and it all felt like a natural progression. As time went on, even Smiddy seemed to have warmed up to her.

Smiddy decided to relocate Love in Action from San Rafael, California, to Memphis, Tennessee, in December of 1994. My last appearance in Sacramento, before we left, was at a large Baptist church. My fiancée and her entire family came out that Sunday evening to show their support. They beamed from the front row as I shared my testimony of change and confessed my love for their daughter. They, like I, marveled at the work of God in my life and were supportive of my decision to marry their child, believing God had great plans for our lives.

In December of that year my fiancée loaded all of her possessions into a moving van, put her old cat in the car with us, and we headed across the country to start our new life in a new town. With God on our side, and our desire to minister to the hurting and broken, we felt nothing could stop us. Unfortunately, disillusionment wasn't far behind.

~ 5 ~
A New Reality

LOVE IN ACTION found a wealthy host church, which paid to move the ministry to Memphis. They helped us rent and renovate office space that was much nicer than the place we rented in San Rafael. A decorator was provided to help us choose colors, furniture and carpet. We each got our own offices, fully decorated and styled in warm Southern charm. There was something about the South that I loved and that made me feel so comfortable. Perhaps it was growing up with parents from the mid-west and family roots from the South. I was certainly familiar with Southern cooking. My grandparents lived just hours away in Oklahoma City. Other relatives lived around us in Arkansas, North Carolina and West Virginia. Nashville, Music City, was a mere four hours away. This felt like destiny.

The churches and buildings around us were gorgeous with brick facade and grand columns. A roommate and I found a large, by California standards, townhome where I would live for the next six months, leading up to my marriage. My fiancée lived with one of our female staff members in a nice apartment, not far from the office.

Our host church was a large non-denominational congregation in central Memphis. The church had thousands of members, a large orchestra and a beautiful Steinway piano that sat majestically in the front of the chapel. Dozens of ministries found their home there. The lead pastor built an empire for the lost in Memphis. Our ministry helped round out an array of other organizations, including a drug and alcohol rehabilitation center for teens, a home for young single mothers, and a fledgling Bible College.

We also secured a beautiful new live-in home for our men. The owner had the house rebuilt from the inside out to accommodate the incoming clients. Love in Action was set to expand and thrive in a more conservative environment, potentially becoming more financially stable. California had become too expensive and we felt the political climate change toward our message and ministry. We dubbed Memphis "the promised land."

Our staff seemed to be reaching a new level of maturity. Another staff member had gotten married before we left California and my marriage was pending. We were a family, and our family was growing. With the changes, John felt the pressure of the board to produce results. And with that, Love In Action began going through modifications in the way the program was run.

Settling In

I began to see John differently than I had in the past. I started to feel as if he was out for his own benefit. From my perspective, he was more interested in building a comfortable middle-class life for himself and his wife, something he couldn't afford in California, and less interested in us as a staff. At one point we as a staff asked for raises because our family situations had changed. Our requests were denied, even though John's financial situation seemed to keep getting better. I didn't know the full story, but I was sure we were getting jilted somewhere in the negotiations.

A sister ministry at our host church had a thriving drug and alcohol recovery program for adolescents. John felt that the 12-step model worked so well for them he would adopt it as an approach to work with recovering homosexuals. Our staff doubted the effectiveness of the new style of ministry, as it was more detached and less personal than the 'successful' Bible-based program Frank Worthen had built. Our wives were virtually removed from any contact with the men. This entire model seemed counterproductive for a ministry built on nurturing relationships. Again, I felt our concerns were pushed aside as John made seemingly independent decisions about the changes.

Much of my time now focused on writing and editing our newsletter. I enjoyed the writing, but missed the interaction and travel that inspired me to write. More and more frequently, I was asked to participate in counseling sessions and to help out with the live-in program. Not only did I not know the men in the program, our interactions were clinical, if not sterile, and my heart simply wasn't in it. I began feeling defeated both personally and in the ministry. My discontentment translated to those who contacted the ministry for help.

Stephen lived in West Memphis, Arkansas. He was excited to find an ex-gay ministry so close to his house, just over the state line. He was married and desperate to talk with someone about his same-sex attraction. Our in-house counselor was unavailable when he called so he got me, instead.

"I don't know what to do," he said, pouring out his heart. "If my wife finds out I'm gay, she'll divorce me." I was familiar with this scenario. It was as common in the South as BBQ and grits. Men were tortured with the conflict between their deeply held religious beliefs and same-sex attractions. Many of them acted out in anonymous sexual encounters in the Southern underground of gay bars. His shame was intense. Still, I struggled to pay attention. It was the same story, different day.

"Listen," I said at the end of the hour, "our main counselor will be back next week. I think you should set up an appointment with him. He is better suited to help you."

"You mean I have to tell this story all over again?" Stephen asked. It had been hard enough to say it once.

"Yes. I'm sorry," I told him. I don't usually counsel people. I'm just here in his absence. I can give you suggestions for what to do, but I think the other person is your best bet." Stephen was not happy with me.

"I don't have time for this," he said. Clearly discouraged, he got out of his chair and reached for the handle on the door. "I just wish you had told me that you weren't the counselor and I would have waited."

I felt bad for Stephen, but more frustrated that I had been put in that position. The ministry began to feel more and more like prison. I wasn't doing what I was hired to do. I certainly didn't want to be counseling anyone.

Premarital Promise

The time my fiancée and I shared together was pleasant enough, but she had a difficult time getting along with her roommate, my co-worker. This made for some awkward conversations at work.

"That's great that you're standing up for your her," Debbie yelled at me, "but this is crap! You don't know what she's like and how she acts toward me." It didn't matter. The girl Debbie despised was going to be my wife. As far as I was concerned, she could do no wrong. Besides, it became apparent that Debbie had emotional issues of her own. It wasn't long before she was asked to leave the ministry.

I had prayed for months for God's direction about my relationship with my fiancée, wanting to make sure I was doing the right thing. Like my parents, I only wanted to be married one time. I felt sure in my decision in spite of those two, what I considered, ill-advised warnings.

One night, shortly before my bachelor party I lay in bed and began to cry. Unlike the other ex-gay weddings I'd attended, which were filled with family and friends, pomp and circumstance, our wedding would be small. I felt alone and distant. My Love in Action co-workers made up most of my bachelor party and it wasn't that I didn't love them, but we didn't really hang out outside of work. I wondered if they really wanted to be there or if they felt obligated, or sorry for me. I felt sorry for myself. I wasn't able to see the blessing of the relationship my father and I had built, or be thankful for my friends. Maybe I'd earned it, having cut so many people out of my life. Either way, I felt alone and lonely. I cried myself to sleep that night, knowing I'd feel better in the morning. I'd had many nights like this in the past. None of them made the others any easier.

My friend Ken hosted my bachelor party, which was full of encouraging words, laughter and affirmation. I was acutely aware that most of the people there weren't going to be lifetime friends, but I managed to enjoy myself anyway, and accept the moment for what it was.

"Before we end tonight," Ken said, "I'd like to have a time of prayer over Tim." Each man prayed for me and then Ken felt he had a word from God for my father. "Dave, I feel the Lord is saying that you will hold your grandchildren in your lap, and that you, your children, and your grandchildren will be blessed through this marriage." That message was even more significant because my father had just come through surgery after being diagnosed with colon cancer. He was about to start chemotherapy. God was also saying that he would live to see my kids. I believed the message confirmed the marriage was ordained and blessed by God, and that God had big plans for our lives.

Wedded Bliss

The wedding was performed in the church where I had been a music minister and where so many things had happened in my life seemingly to lead me away from that moment. It was a testimony to the power of God and the defeat of the enemy. The Scripture we chose and imprinted on our wedding bulletin said:

They will be called oaks of righteousness, a planting of the Lord for the display of his splendor." Isaiah 61:3 (NIV)

I wasn't nervous; in fact I felt rather confident. My bride was beautiful and the ceremony went off without a hitch. We had so many people attend our wedding there was barely any room to sit.

The next day we boarded a plane to Maui for our honeymoon and then headed to San Diego for a week-long Exodus International Conference. I taught two classes, one on leadership and one on youth ministry. As newly weds, we were the hit of the conference, and it seemed like everyone knew who we were.

"Congratulations!" Sy Rogers yelled from across the campus where he stood with his wife. We were welcomed and hugged by John and Anne Paulk, Frank and Anita Worthen, Bob Davies, and another Love in Action couple, whose wedding we had attended just months earlier. It felt good to be loved and to be noticed. We were examples of what could happen to people who simply followed the will of God and allowed him to heal their innermost thoughts and desires.

Soon the week ended and we flew back to Memphis where we had purchased a house. It was the first time we'd live in it together. The idea of building a home with my wife was exciting. Within a few months we got a dog and named him Bob Buford. The name had a Southern ring to it that resonated with where we lived and where we were at that time in our lives. Buford, I discovered later, was also my grandfather's middle name. It was just more confirmation, in my mind, that we were where we were supposed to be.

Trouble in Paradise

To say our marriage was difficult is an understatement. Expectations were not being met on a number of levels. Additionally, the media events and outreach programs had dried up in our new hometown.

I was confined to the office even more, and more involved with the live-in program than I had ever been. I spent countless hours running groups and Bible studies, and listening to the men's problems.

My new wife was nothing like my mother, and she was depressed after moving away from her family and friends. I was unaware of the impact her abusive past experiences, and growing up in an alcoholic home, had on our relationship. Her contentious attacks and provocations over something as simple as keeping the house clean were a mystery to me. I had never been an angry person before, but found myself reacting almost violently toward her. We were frequently embattled over emotional control of our relationship. I assumed most of the responsibility of our problems because I saw them as results of my struggles with same-sex attraction. My wife was content to let me take the blame.

We sought church counseling, which seemed to confirm my suspicions that the problems were due to my inability to relate to her mentally and sexually. It grew increasingly evident that she wanted more from our relationship than I was able to give. In those rare moments of emotional honesty she confided, "It's almost like there is an invisible wall between us and I can't get to the other side." I felt defeated. I was failing as a husband.

Our house was constantly messy, which added to the feeling of being out of control of my circumstances and emotions. To make matters worse, she hated her job and the misogyny of the Southern men with whom she worked. She had difficulty making friends and took issue with Love in Action's leaders and their decisions that impacted our lives.

One night we were supposed to attend our host church's function to honor the pastor who brought the ministry to Memphis. My wife decided not to go and I was forced to decide to attend without her or stay home. Exhausted from the constant conflict, I yielded to the pressure from her to stay, but simultaneously felt guilty for flaking out on an obligation. "No one will even miss us," she told me.

Over at the Smid's house later that week John asked, "Where were you two Sunday night? Jimmy was asking about you." Jimmy was the Senior Pastor of the church who was honored at the event.

"My wife wasn't feeling well," I told John, "and we decided not to go."

Visibly angry, John said, "Well, you should have gone; I felt embarrassed that you weren't there to represent the ministry." His voice was shaking.

"You know what, John," my wife shouted back. "You don't own us. I wasn't feeling well and you aren't even showing any concern for me or for us. If Tim was required to go, then you should have told him this was a required event!"

I wasn't used to conflict, at least not blatant conflict. A rift was developing between John and me. I saw my wife as a huge part of the problem. She was draining me. I wondered what I was doing wrong and prayed about how to fix it. We became increasingly unhappy with each other.

I felt like my wife's constant demands, usually unspoken, were crushing my desire to serve in the ministry. I had to make more and more choices between my job and her. She wasn't working with me like the ministry partner I envisioned. My unhappiness with my job was only exacerbated by my marriage. I was in a vicious cycle of discontentment.

Seeking to find my place away from Love in Action and become more "normal," I applied for, and was hired as, a music minister at a small Memphis church. The congregation welcomed us with open arms. It seemed a good place for us to call home and we found friends and a sense of belonging. They treated me like a rock star and I reveled in the attention and quality musicianship this little Memphis church held.

Love in Action continued to change, as did John. Neither John nor I was happy at this point, and both of us felt it was time for me to leave. I found a day job at Youth for Christ as a Development Director. I worked primarily for one hard-nosed board member who pushed me beyond my capacity to raise money like one of the sales guys at his financial firm. I was there for a miserable seven months. Though the people I worked with were well aware of my involvement with ex-gay ministry, it was seldom the topic of conversation. I learned that the subject of homosexuality was off-limits in the office and, in a sense, I was forced back into hiding any thoughts or feelings. Homosexuality was generally a topic only whispered about in the South outside of ex-gay ministry. Working to alleviate it was one thing, but living with it was quite another.

Now, I was learning to navigate in the real world, away from any support of ex-gay ministry. My desire for "normalcy" wasn't meeting my expectation. I could relate to other married couples, but I knew – even if I didn't admit it – that there was a layer to my relationship they didn't have. I kept my thoughts to myself and pretended to be like everyone else.

By 1997, my only ministry involvement was with our Memphis congregation. I found a secular job, which paid much better than the ministry jobs I'd been doing for the past six years. I felt more financially secure, but that was all. I didn't feel much of a purpose. All the excitement of the media and traveling slowly became a distant memory. I assumed that this was my testing ground. God led me to this place and I needed to learn how to live a "normal" married life. I was disappointed that things weren't working out as I'd hoped.

A New Normal

In spite of it all, my wife and I tried to have children. Never having had much of a paternal instinct, I was content with our lack of immediate results, but my wife was persistent. A medical diagnosis and procedure resolved the problem and resulted in pregnancy with our first child. The mood of our house changed. The pregnancy drew us closer and, for the first time in two years, we were getting along. I read the Bible to my unborn child every night. Knowing that I was going to be a father brought renewed hope that maybe there was a purpose to my life after all. I needed to be patient and see what God would do.

I continued working my corporate job, moved into management, and eventually created a training department. The money increased but staying in Memphis for a job seemed less important after having a child. Our daughter's grandparents lived in California. My wife wanted to leave the comfortable life we had created in Memphis and move back there. I wasn't completely convinced, but after five years of fighting with her, watching her struggle with depression and trying to build and maintain relationships, I decided it was best. Additionally, I had become increasingly unhappy with the level of racism where we lived. Reverse discrimination was a problem in my own neighborhood, and even I felt unfairly treated. I didn't want to raise my child under those circumstances.

I looked for new ministry opportunities in California and was eventually offered a job as a music minister in Sacramento. It seemed like the perfect position in the perfect location, so in December of 1999, we put our home on the market and moved back to Sacramento. Emotionally, I was exhausted from the politics of ministry, but I had high hopes for finding my way back to the spiritual high and sense of purpose I had experienced a few years earlier.

The friction between my wife and me returned and, over time, took its toll. I resented her for not doing her part to help raise our child. She loved to play with the baby, but didn't seem to take much interest in changing diapers, feeding her on a schedule, or taking care of her as most mothers did. Her sister moved in with us to be our nanny, despite my opposition. I didn't see a need for a third adult to raise a single child. For some reason, however, the task seemed to overwhelm the new mother. My bitterness mounted.

Everything for us was a battle. I didn't want to be married anymore, but like being gay, divorce wasn't an option. Death: now that was an option. This time, though, it wasn't *myself* I wanted to kill, it was her. If she died, I figured, my life would be better. Of course, I couldn't be the one to do it, so I'd just have to pray and hope that somehow God would hear me. The conflict she brought into the marriage was now mine and I'd learned to cope by emotionally disconnecting, spending hours with pornography and doing anything to avoid her.

We lived with my parents for several months while waiting for our Memphis house to sell and our new house to be built. Our entire family – two dogs, one cat, and a baby– squeezed into a single bedroom. Her sister moved back home with her parents. In spite of our uncomfortable situation, and the fact that sex was almost nonexistent between us, we conceived our second daughter.

One More Time

I wasn't prepared for the backward ways of the pastor at our new church. In our haste to leave Memphis we didn't research him enough to know that his old-fashioned Pentecostal beliefs found demons in every Pokémon. Like my church upbringing, he overly-spiritualized everything and determined the level of a person's relationship with God by how emotional he or she sounded when praying. Later he would tell me I didn't sound like I had a relationship with God at all.

During the hiring process he said, "I'm not going to tell you to show off, but when you play for the congregation pull out all the stops and show them what you can do." He and the congregation seemed pleased with my urban Gospel style. I felt fortunate to find a racially-mixed congregation that allowed me to play the way I knew how, without the judgmental eye of some of the white people I'd encountered in congregations in the past for playing "rock-n-roll." Still, I was tired. Music, which had always been my spiritual connection, now felt forced.

My first few weeks on the new job were exceptionally uncomfortable. I'd lost my voice due to a bad cold and relied on others to lead worship. The pastor held me to unspoken and unrealistic expectations to have a worship experience created by their last music minister. I also learned that harmony and vocal riffs, were labeled "showboating." The pastor called out those who did such things as self-serving exhibitionists, who took glory from God. The same did not hold true for his exuberant and often overly dramatic style of preaching.

Mondays at my new church became especially difficult. Week after week the pastor pulled me in his office to tell me what I had done wrong: I didn't hold the crescendo long enough during prayer time, or I didn't give the Holy Spirit enough time to move during the service. He finally decided that he would create the list of songs himself, so we could practice how it was to be done prior to the services. I finally realized the problem was that I wasn't playing the piano the way his wife played. In spite of his multi-cultural congregation he wanted the music to represent *his* culture.

One Sunday morning, while preparing the choir for the service, the pastor showed up in the doorway of the choir room visibly angry. "What did you do?" he said sternly to me in front of my choir. The room grew quiet. I walked into the hall to find out what he was talking about. "My wife is out there crying because of something you said to her. What did you say to make her so upset?! You need to go apologize right now!"

It turned out she was unhappy with a last minute change and she simply didn't have the skills to pull it off. She complained to her husband who felt addressing the problem right before the service was as good a time as any. He had little self-control over his anger.

While the worship became regulated, I poured my efforts into the choir and it grew exponentially in a short time. The fresh breath of new music excited choir members and the congregation. People who left the choir came back. I encouraged people with musical talent to show it off. Worship, in my opinion, meant using one's talent to the best of his or her abilities. The senior pastor soon had had enough.

"If I wanted a black music minister I would have hired one!" he yelled one Monday morning. "Enough is enough. It's been three months and I'm giving you the choice to resign or be fired. I've written your resignation letter and all you have to do is sign it. You have one week to decide."

Just as I hit a new low in my ministry career I received a letter from a renowned Nashville choir. A song I'd submitted to them to record had been rejected. My wife, knowing my mental state, hid the letter from me, but I found it. "We like the song," it said, "but would like for you to re-work the lyrics." In another frame of mind I would have been excited by the promise, but all I saw was rejection. I wasn't good enough, again.

My musical career had fizzled. Ministry, all I had known for years, was disintegrating. My wife was pregnant and we were buying a house. I had no job prospects and the only education I had was an associate's degree in liberal arts. I had no training other than administrative work and mortgage banking. More than ever, I felt my life spinning out of control.

In desperation I got my real estate license and decided to become a loan officer. The future was uncertain, but I saw a glimmer of hope when my wife, six months pregnant, landed a job just weeks before we signed the paperwork for our new house. Three months later our second daughter was born.

Unlike the first pregnancy, where we found common ground, we lacked any sort of support. The preceding months of change and insecurity hacked away at the remaining threads of our relationship. Another baby and less money made life even more stressful. I was a man without a purpose. My glory days were behind me at 35 years old. We stopped attending church altogether. The last experience left a bitter taste in our mouths and we grew to distrust pastors in general. Besides, getting two babies ready and going to church, especially when we didn't *have* to be there, was taxing.

God grew more distant than ever. I was angry with Him for allowing me to be in this situation. My wife was uncontrollable, rebellious and lacked any spiritual maturity to make good decisions. I spent more and more time on the Internet searching gay porn sites, feeling justified because my wife wasn't interested in me and God was silent, despite my prayers.

The conversations between my wife and me grew more volatile. Any sexual attraction I had for her was gone. I was bitter and hopeless. Simple discussions were fodder for a battle of control over the other person. She found fault in everything I did and I resented everything she said.

When I attempted to get us into counseling, she merely told me that I needed to deal with *my* problems. Her inability, or outright refusal, to take responsibility for our relationship only left the option to live our miserable lives out together, until fate, I hoped, would remove her permanently. I was determined to make sure she was just as miserable as I was and ensured as much with spiteful and hurtful words. The consequences of my behavior completely blindsided me.

− 6 −

SIX YEARS OF SILENCE

AFTER ANOTHER HUGE fight, Thanksgiving Day 2001, I stormed out of our house and drove to our friends' house, just down the street. My gut told me this fight triggered an outcome for which I was not prepared. "I think she's about to divorce me," I told my friend Josh. Josh stared at me uncomfortably for a moment. He was one of the groomsmen at our wedding. His wife was my wife's matron of honor. I sat there taking in the words I had uttered, as though someone else said them. I felt a mixture of shock, disgust, anger, bitterness and relief. I didn't want a divorce; I just wanted peace.

Josh and his wife had uncomfortably watched the relationship between my wife and me dissolve from the beginning. We had such high hopes for all of us getting together once we moved back to California, but our best intentions left us more secluded from one another.

I stayed at Josh and Rachel's house until the last possible moment, eventually making my way home to greet our holiday visitors. The tension between my wife and me was obvious. I interpreted even simple requests from her as an underlying motive to assert control over me. She had to have it; I couldn't give it up.

Once the last guest left, we sat in our family room, now full of empty chairs and card tables draped in festive tablecloths that were covered in crumbs and wadded-up napkins. We were both exhausted. I stared at the yellow wall behind her. I didn't want to deal with any of this. The disheveled tables and after-dinner mess metaphorically represented where our relationship had been for years. The party was over. We waited too long to deal with the disorder we had created. Perhaps it wasn't impossible to clean, but neither of us had the energy to try anymore.

Both of us folded our arms and prepared for another war of words. Not to be disappointed, the next half hour we screamed and berated each other over the day's events. Like all of the fights in the past, this one went nowhere. There was no resolution. No one backed down. Both of us had hit a brick wall. We sat for several minutes in silence.

Finally, she uttered the words I'd dichotomously expected to hear and never saw coming. "I want a divorce," she said. Her emotions were gone. Her heart was cold. The hatred I felt for her overcame any feelings of sadness I otherwise might have had. All that was wrong with my life sat in the form of a person in front of me. *She* ruined my ministry career; *she* ruined any chance at happiness, and now *she* would destroy our children by divorcing me.

Later that night my mind raced as I contemplated what the future might look like. *Would we really get divorced?* I wondered. It's simply something Christians don't do. My mind mostly went to my children. I couldn't even imagine life for *my* children coming from a broken home. The thought was incomprehensible. *It would be better for them to be dead than to live in separate homes*, I contemplated. *It would be better for all of us to be dead.* I allowed myself to think of even dark alternatives rather than let her destroy my family in this way.

The awkwardness of our relationship took hold as we both resumed living in a house we each wanted the other to leave. Within the next few weeks I realized she had begun an emotional affair with someone at work before we spoke of our separation. Her decision to divorce me wasn't as sudden as it appeared. She began spending more nights away from home, leaving me alone with our infant and toddler daughters, who frequently asked where their mother was. As if it were possible, my hatred of this woman grew. I felt betrayed and deceived. I was disgusted with her lack of moral judgment. I was heartbroken for the effects and the legacy it left for our children. *How could I have been so stupid?* I asked myself.

Looking at Life Alone

God seemed to disappear from the chaos that had become my life. I had believed Him to be the spiritual, emotional and moral compass of my journey, so why would He allow me to marry someone He knew would be an adulteress? Why would He allow such tragedy to happen to my family? If He loved my wife and my kids more than I did, why did He, if He *truly* had the power to change or fix this, allow it to happen? I was consumed with unanswerable questions. Struggling with unwanted same-sex attraction was more than enough for one person to bear. To let me go through such horrific pain as a father and husband felt cruel. My heart had been crushed.

My emotional and spiritual states spiraled out of control. Depression and suicide enveloped me. Each day became perfunctory. I operated in a daze. The armor of perfection wasn't just cracking, it was crumbling, and the humiliation of my failures screamed for attention.

As in times past, I cut people out of my life by simply disappearing. I'd stopped responding to phone calls, letters and emails. This time, I felt especially shameful about going through a divorce. The fact that she cheated and initiated the divorce offered some solace. I took every opportunity to point out her faults, her decisions and her behaviors as the source of our problems. Still, I couldn't escape the fact that my life, built on the perception of the perfect Christian family, was a lie. Every interaction with people highlighted, in my mind, that I was a disappointment to humankind.

"Hey, Tim," my boss Mitchell called to me as I walked by his office. I worked as a loan officer at a mortgage company at the time.

"Hi, Mitchell," I forced a smile and paused at his door.

"Do you have a couple of minutes? I need to go over this file with you," he said. Neither he nor I was prepared for what happened next. "Go ahead and shut the door, if you don't mind." I mechanically shut the door behind me and sat in a side chair against the wall in Mitchell's office.

With little more than eye contact I broke down sobbing. I knew the walls were thin enough for people to hear me and it didn't take long before people walked by the partially open blinds to see what was going on. The perfectly coiffed image of self-confidence and Christian family values melted away in a flood of tears. Mitchell got up from behind his desk and awkwardly held me in his arms. "She's divorcing me," I confessed inconsolably.

"I am so sorry," Mitchell said, trying his best to comfort an employee with whom he had a mostly formal relationship. We stood there for several minutes. I tried to pull it together and Mitchell tried to figure out how to make it stop. "Why don't you take the day off? Go do what you need to do and let me know what I can do to help," he encouraged me. "I'll take care of your files."

I left the office that day with nowhere to go. Home reminded me of the horrible failure that was my family life. That weekend my wife was moving out and taking the kids with her. I knew I needed to fight for my kids, but was rendered emotionally impotent. I felt I would never recover from this. There was no future for me, or my children.

That night I rented a hotel room and contemplated how to put an end to the pain. After several hours of watching TV, I decided to cruise some bookstores for pornography. I could spend hours looking through racks of magazines and videos. It helped me forget everything else. This time was different, though. At the end of a long night I still ended up alone in a hotel, still empty, and still devastated by the agony. I grew numb.

For several months my now estranged wife had tried to get me to leave our home. I refused. Since she initiated the divorce, I reasoned, she was the one who needed to leave. The following day was the day she moved out, taking most of what we had in the house. The experience of knowing she would be gone when I got back was surreal. It was Saturday morning. I left the hotel room and just began to drive.

I thought how the pain in my life never really went away, but in fact only grew worse. The few months of respite seemed nothing more than a breeding ground for more pain. If God saw it, He didn't care enough to do something about it. I waited until my parents left their house. I knew they had obligations during the day and when they were gone I would grab my father's gun and end my life.

My kids were young enough, I reasoned, that if I killed myself it wouldn't be as painful and they would never know what they missed.

I made my way into my parents' house and rummaged through their drawers and closets until I found the box where they kept their guns. It was locked. I frantically searched for the key. After nearly 30 years in their home they had accumulated an impressively large collection of keys in nightstands, kitchen drawers, dresser drawers and key holders. None of them worked. "Goddammit!" I cursed. "Why is everything I do so damn hard!" I was filled with rage, despair and desperation. I screeched out of their driveway and began driving again. Anywhere. Nowhere.

The pain of my childhood and early adult years paled in comparison to what I experienced now with children in the picture. All of these experiences culminated into what I always thought of myself growing up: I'm a colossal failure. I was incapable of love or being loved. Like a burn victim I was disfigured. I felt ugly, exposed, and inconsolable. I sensed that people were staring at me, judging me, pitying me and never giving me the chance to explain, defend myself or offer a reason. What was the reason, anyway? I didn't have an answer.

I drove around sobbing, practically unable to see through the tears. Finally able to release the pent up emotion, I was simultaneously drawn to suicide and the responsibility to stay and raise my children. I knew the emotional pain, somehow, had to be set aside to nurture them and make them feel loved. They should always feel loved.

THE REALITY OF DIVORCE

The courthouse was a beautiful building. I'd never so much as filed a police report, so standing inside the majestic stone structure amid others' court papers of domestic violence, drug and alcohol abuse and child protective services was a world far from my own. If ever there was an evil presence in my life, this was it. I felt like I was in the devil's territory. *Christians don't belong in family court*, I thought. I never saw myself as one of those low-life divorcés who required judicial intervention. I reasoned that the devil wanted to destroy my life and he had a pretty strong grip to take me down, along with my children. His vehicle of choice was my soon-to-be ex-wife.

My mother-in-law, heartbroken over the divorce of her daughter, became my ally. She believed, like I did, that there was a heavenly battle raging against our family. The only way to fix our situation was through earnest and heartfelt prayer. "Here," she said, "I have a couple of books I want you to read on spiritual warfare."

I read voraciously, something I didn't normally do. I was looking for answers and holding out hope that somehow my altered state of reality would snap back into place. It was the place where God healed emotions, cured homosexuality, and His will mirrored traditional American family life. I prayed God would deliver my ex-wife from her life of promiscuity and give her a heart for her children. I prayed she would see the error of her ways and come back home. I prayed God would once and for all deliver me from my homosexual desires, and replace them with an even more powerful testimony of change and forgiveness. I believed He would make my family a shining example of what His power can do.

I took suicide off the table and threw myself back into church. I needed to feel God's presence if I was ever going to get through this. We had attended a church near our home a couple of times, so I was aware of a racially-mixed congregation where I felt most comfortable.

After going there for a few months I approached the music minister and asked to play the organ, a Hammond B3, the quintessential instrument in black Gospel music. Dale, the music minister, had a history in the Church of God in Christ, was an amazing musician in his own right and seemed eager to work with me. Simultaneously, the church had launched an ex-gay ministry and I thought getting involved would reignite my passion and put me back on the right path.

I stayed in the background of the church, avoiding any kind of leadership position. I didn't feel worthy to lead anyone or anything. Sitting in front of the choir while they learned their parts and I played was awkward enough. I didn't want to be seen. Making friendships was difficult because I didn't feel valuable enough to be a friend to anyone. I wasn't worth anyone's time, and I thought I would probably just screw up their lives anyway.

Going back into music took me back to my roots. In my early days of ministry I had learned to pay attention to responses, strike the right chord, punctuate the preacher and take the crowd on a spiritual journey into repentance, thanksgiving, or praise. I felt led of the Holy Spirit. It was my calling. It was my connection to heaven.

Now my emotions were raw. I desperately wanted to feel the guidance I once had and see God heal my marriage. I still held out hope that it was possible. While it felt good to be a part of musical magic at this church, something had changed in me. I was dead at the core. I didn't see God's anointing; I saw responses to the music simply as human emotion.

Somewhere the mysticism had dissipated. I started to notice secular musicians could do what I did without any spiritual connotation. At the end of the day, nothing really changed in people's lives. The ministry I had built for 25 years seemed suddenly empty. I looked back and thought of all the choirs, music groups, concerts and worship services I'd directed. I received compliments, notes and letters of how people were blessed, but their lives were never *really* changed, at least not permanently. Neither was mine. *Perhaps music had nothing to do with God after all*, I thought.

Reality began sinking into my once unshakable belief that the Bible was the inerrant Word of God. And perhaps, God was not in control. I couldn't deny that things looked and felt differently. My heart had been broken and the musical balm that once served as a cure for all that ailed me no longer worked. I was forced, against my will, into an existence different than the one I wanted to see.

As the months ticked by it became apparent that my ex-wife was never coming back. I wondered why I was praying for her to change. I wondered why, if she had free will, I was praying for her at all. In my understanding of Scripture, He would never force her to do anything she didn't want to do.

Spiritual warfare didn't make sense after all. If what Jesus did on the cross broke the power of Satan over our lives, wasn't the victory already won? Life seemed harder than it was supposed to be, if I understood my Scriptures correctly. After all, what glory was God getting out of this? Why would He need to make an example of my life if He is omnipotent? In the great scheme of things, my life is unimportant and insignificant. Why would the devil care whether my family was whole? Or even if I was gay? Did God's reputation depend on this? Did my decisions or actions really make a difference?

Why was I trying so hard if God didn't care to change anything? Unanswered questions shot through my mind like a machine gun.

SINGLE AGAIN

On December 19, 2002, my divorce was final. It was over. I was relieved to be done with the drama, but somewhat despondent. I'd spent the last year closing the last doors on friendships. The shame of failure was too much. I was reminded of it with every conversation, even though no one brought it up. I felt people's disappointments and was sure it was on the forefronts of their minds.

At church I became that sad, divorced man who quietly sat in the pew. I'd seen a lot of these people in my church career. They'd go through divorce and have trouble finding a place to fit in. Church is mostly about couples, marriage and building families. Single people are carted off into separate rooms where a nice young couple ministers to them with Bible studies and pithy comments about how God has a plan for their lives. They are never really included in the mainstream culture. I was now one of them. It was something else to remind me that I was different and not really accepted.

My father became my source of companionship and we talked frequently throughout the week. I'd tell the same stories, express the same bitterness and he'd listen intently, telling me everything would work out. My father was my go-to person and confidant. When I decided to jump back on the no-pornography wagon I asked him to keep me accountable. Unfortunately, it only added to the shame when I had to admit that I failed again and again.

I had remained involved with my church for three more years and attended the ex-gay support group. Whatever friendships I made there, however, remained mostly superficial. The rhetoric of change had grown tiring. I had gone from a leader in the movement to a mere participant ten years later, hiding my identity. Once again I found myself in a sub-sub-Christian culture, meeting in a non-descript breakroom of a mega church. I was no further along and life wasn't getting better.

Now, at 38 years old, I was alone and responsible for two more lives. Midlife approached fast and furiously, but nothing turned out the way I expected at that age. The only skills I had were speaking and singing. No respectable church would have me. Besides, I didn't even know what was true anymore.

For the next several years I went to work, and I came home. I put 50 pounds on my small frame, reaching nearly 200 pounds. I desperately wanted the pain to end, but I knew my children needed me. Now growing older and becoming more aware of their surroundings, I couldn't stand the thought of the devastation they would experience if someone had to tell them, "Daddy's dead." Nevertheless, I kept the suicide fantasy alive. Mentally acting out the steps of pulling the trigger helped me fall sleep at night.

Mindless Decisions

In 2004, I got a job as a trainer with a large mortgage company. I was again in front of audiences as I traveled from city to city teaching classes, though the topics were less than motivating and the crowds were much smaller. Six months into the job, my manager, Randy, told me it was time for a review. "I want you to fill this form out," he said, "and I'll sign it." I struggled through the paperwork, trying to decide what I was good at, which felt like nothing, and what needed improvement. Finally, I turned in my paperwork. Randy and I reviewed it together.

"Ok," he said. "I can agree with most of this. You said you are going to improve your skills by going to school?"

"That's what I said," I told Randy matter-of-factly.

"Which school?" he asked.

"Um, I don't know," I said. "I travel quite a bit, as you know, so I'm not even sure how to do that."

"There are several good schools out there," Randy prodded. "I'll write you a recommendation letter and do what I can to help you find the right one. When do you plan to start?"

I felt cornered. I really didn't plan to start at all. I thought the objective was to simply fill out the review, turn it in, and get a raise. His persistence was a little annoying. Still, Randy had a good heart. He wasn't much older than me, but presented himself as a wise-old sage. All of his employees saw him that way. "This fall?" I said with less confidence.

"Great. Check into the schools and come back to me next week," he told me.

Well, this is a quandary, I thought. *I just got a mandate to go to school.* I searched online for schools to see what the options were and then brought them to Randy at our next meeting.

"Yep, that looks good," Randy said. "Here's your reference letter." Almost mindlessly, I gathered my transcripts and applied for school. Soon, my evenings in the hotel went from watching TV to writing papers and doing research. Something in my brain clicked. *If I can research questions about business topics like ethics and marketing, I can just as easily research questions about Christianity, homosexuality, and psychology,* I thought. For several years I'd wondered how I turned out to be this way. Biblical answers weren't sufficient anymore, and I was amazed at how much information was online. I began a journey that would ultimately change everything for me.

New Possibilities

Like shaking the Magic Eight Ball I typed, "Is God real?" into the search bar on my laptop one night. It was a question I'd pondered in the back of my mind, but never had the audacity to ask aloud. I was looking for proof, archeological digs, empirical evidence of healings, or anything to give me a reason to keep holding on. I wasn't looking for an escape, but for validation. I spent hours reading articles, re-reading books at home, reading my Bible and finally asking the tough questions:

> Why does the Bible contradict itself if it's the inerrant word of God?

> What is it about the Bible and Christianity that agnostics and atheists disagree with?

> Are there interpretations of the Bible, other than the ones I was raised to believe, that make sense?

> Why don't most Jews believe in Christianity?

> How do we know the virgin birth is true?

> How do scientists explain the flood, Noah's Ark, and Jesus's life?

I'd read apologetical books on the topics, Christian authors who offered a defense or reason that fit within the guidelines of the faith, but their reasoning was more directed at keeping belief in tact than actually answering the questions. The answers didn't consider anything else other than the Bible. I needed definitive answers this time. I could no longer accept that God's ways were higher than my ways and I simply wasn't able to understand. I had determined that either it was all true, or none of it was true.

One search on Noah's ark was particularly poignant. I read that the remains of the ark were found on Mt. Ararat and Christians pointed to this as proof of the flood. Further research stated that the fossils found by archeologists were certainly not Noah's famed ark and offered an explanation for what they discovered. "Huh," I said sitting alone at my laptop, "it's really all about perspective." It was the first time in my fundamentalist upbringing that I realized what we consider truth is really based on how we interpret it. Further searches and studies led me to understand that interpretations about events not only depend on the outcome, but how the question is framed by the person asking. In other words, asking a question like, "What proof is there that the Bible is the Word of God?" begins with the presumption that the Bible is the Word of God. If I believed the Bible to be the true, inerrant Word of God and the God of the Bible to be who I thought He was, evidence pointed me back to my initial belief. But what if it was something else? What if I *didn't* believe that to be the case? The answers pointed me in an entirely different direction.

Back home I spent more time with my kids than the custody agreement allotted and I assumed all the responsibilities of a single parent. I found fulfillment as a dad, though the underlying emptiness and failure never left me. It ran deep and inconsolable. My small house became enormous when the girls weren't with me. I worried about them. I knew my ex-in-laws were there to pick up where their mother left off, but it didn't help relieve the heartache of not being there to tuck them in at night and wake them in the morning.

Away from the girls and on the road, school became my passion. I enjoyed the intense discussions particularly about ethics. I managed to turn class conversations toward human behavior. My major was business management, but my passion was psychology. Of course, the deeper, burning question for me was how I turned out to be gay?

I focused on schoolwork when I needed to, but pondered the more life-impacting inquiries that hounded my brain. I never imagined life without God, without church, without the culture in which everything I believed to be true didn't exist. What would my parents think if I suddenly took a turn? What would life look like for me? This was an option I had never considered. The prospect was too scary. I'd made my living in the ministry and spent years of my life in church. Now I was in a different place and found an opportunity to look at things differently without the risk of losing my livelihood. Moreover, I was at a crossroads and it was time for something different.

Life wasn't working for me. I wanted to believe, but I was tired. I knew, hearing occasionally from friends in the ex-gay ministry, that their lives were not as they appeared. In fact, by this point all the world knew that my former Love in Action co-worker, John Paulk, was caught in a gay bar way back in 2001. I assumed that since the ex-gay thing wasn't working for me, it wasn't working for John, but I didn't have enough self-confidence to check with John. I assumed he was doing much better than me. Still, enough doubt about my view of the Gospel existed that my entire belief system was in question.

An Intellectual Journey

In 2004 I abruptly "retired" from music and left the church. I boxed up my recording studio, instruments and songbooks and quit everything. The church had been going through a transition and some of the musicians were leaving with one of the pastors. It seemed like a good time to exit. Without saying a word, like I'd done many times before in past relationships, I simply disappeared. Metaphorically, boxing up my music was like boxing up my relationship with God and shoving it all in the attic. I didn't even realize that quitting music meant I would quit feeling. I vanished into an intellectual cocoon where knowledge, devoid of any emotion, set me on a new path and quest for answers.

At this point, nearly five years after our divorce, my ex-wife and I found a comfortable place in our relationship. When she asked to move in for six months so she could save some money I thought it was a good idea. She'd always struggled to save money so I knew she would be with me more than six months. Besides, it brought my kids back home full-time and made my house a lot less empty. With everyone back home, I was less lonely and more confident that my girls were being cared for.

By the time I graduated with my bachelor's degree I had already enrolled in graduate school. My mind was thirsty for knowledge. I chose to go after an education degree because I still believed, at that point, that homosexuality was a learned behavior. I was deeply involved in corporate training and a master's degree in education fit nicely with my career goals.

It was in graduate school I met Sonia, a Hollywood television writer looking to get a master's degree as a backup to a longstanding, but unstable career. For some reason I was drawn to Sonia. I'd always heard that those in higher education were more liberal and less judgmental. Sonia, I assumed, living in Hollywood, working in television *and* involved in higher education, provided a safe place to share my story. "I no longer believe God exists," I told her one night.

"Hang on a minute," she said. "How can you be so certain?"

This was the first time I'd said such a thing aloud to anyone. I figured if anyone were godless, it would be her. If growing up in church taught me nothing else, Hollywood was not a friend of God. They are a blasphemous people, out to destroy the morality, upon which this great country was founded. I was taken aback by her response.

"I go to a Presbyterian Church here in Hollywood," she said. "I absolutely believe God exists and He loves you. Just because life didn't turn out the way you wanted it to doesn't mean God stopped being God. Don't throw the baby out with the bathwater."

Liberal Christians most certainly weren't going to heaven, I was raised to believe, so to have one preach to me about my faith seemed terribly ironic. Yet, somehow I felt compelled to share the rest of my story. I told her all about being ex-gay, or gay, or bi or whatever I was. She didn't seem the least bit concerned. "I still don't see how that changes whether or not God exists and I don't see why it matters to God or anyone else," she assured me.

"But how can you believe the Bible and accept homosexuality?" I asked. I understood pro-gay theology, but it was only used to justify the sin. Sonia was not a lesbian.

"Just because we don't interpret the Bible the way you do doesn't mean we don't accept it to be God's Word," she said. "We just see it differently."

Sonia and I cultivated our friendship over the next year. She told me of her sexual escapades and life raising two daughters as a single mother. It was a life far from my experience as an Evangelical Christian. She didn't have a problem reconciling her life, salty language and all, to her faith. I was raised to believe that swearing was a sin. Even in my newfound state of questioning everything, swearing was off limits to me. I considered her no more saved than a non-Christian, but the companionship felt good. There weren't a lot of people who knew all about me. Those that did were cut off from my life. I was determined to put the past behind me, make new friends and start over, unaware of the floodgate about to be opened.

– 7 –
LOVE, LUST AND BELONGING

WITH MY GIRLS and their mom back in the house, and me focused on school, I was finally ready to explore life outside of the rigid boundaries I'd lived within for over 40 years. I needed to find out what *was* true and what else was out there. Somewhere I'd heard that people could make friends through a website called Craigslist. I thought I'd give it a shot. Six years in hiding started to get old. I needed new friends. Then again, it seemed like I always needed new friends. To say I was naive about Craigslist is an understatement.

I read through the ads on the website, most of which I didn't understand, and some of which shocked me. Nothing in the ads appealed to me so I thought I'd write my own. What I wrote was:

41-year-old man looking for friendship. Divorced. Lonely.

What he must have read was:

Man looking for young Greek God who is smart, funny and can turn my world upside down.

"Hi. I'm Ron," read the email. "I'm a doctoral student at a college in a nearby town. I'm from Hawaii and I have a girlfriend back home. She's in med school. Since I don't live permanently in California, I'm also looking for friends while I'm here."

Ron's honesty was endearing, but he soon started asking questions that seemed out of place, particularly about my sexual orientation. I didn't understand why he automatically presumed I was bisexual. Nevertheless, I answered his questions and asked my own. Ron was also in a transition period; I just didn't know it at the time. For two months we chatted online and emailed each other. I thought it was odd how he responded to my texts and emails so quickly, but I ate up the attention. I was actually turned on by it.

When Ron suggested we meet in person I was ready to find out more about him. I was nervous. I'd never done anything like this. I had stabilized at 200 pounds. I wasn't feeling great about how I looked and I knew I was taking a risk to actually meet a new friend in person. I had all of the 'what-if' questions going through my mind: What if he doesn't like me? What if I'm too old/fat/ugly/uninteresting/stupid for him? But, I needed to take the risk.

I drove into the parking lot of the Starbucks where we agreed to meet. It was an unusually brisk summer afternoon as I stepped out of and stood beside my little Ford Mustang convertible, waiting for Ron to arrive. Soon, I recognized the description of his car and watched him pull into an open space. *What kind of a person drives a toaster,* I thought as I watched him park his blue Scion. From where I stood Ron didn't exactly look like the picture he sent. His hair was long, black and straight. As a Japanese-American doctoral student, he did not match the sterotype I envisioned.

His 5'11" frame came out of the car and even his loose clothing couldn't hide the fact that he was built like a mythological god. His eyes were certainly Asian, but he had a chiseled chin, a smile that could melt a straight guy's heart and a personality to match. If I felt insecure before, I was certainly feeling it then. The only thing chiseled about me was the grip I'd developed on a fork and spoon.

I quickly slipped into "trainer mode." That's where, like Clark Kent, I step into an invisible phone booth and come out acting like a super hero, full of charm, confidence and personality.

Ron was the guy I wanted to be. He was smart, popular at school, came from a wealthy family, and had won awards for his athleticism. His uncertainty about his sexuality wasn't an apparent problem. We spent hours talking in that Starbucks on a busy corner in my hometown. He told me about his girlfriend and how much he loved her, his family life, his passion for health and helping people achieve theirs. His kind eyes mesmerized me.

On one hand I felt like I was talking to an old friend. On the other hand, Ron and I made a connection I had never felt before. He told me he saw something special in me. I needed to hear that. Still reeling from so many failures, Ron validated me. This man who seemed to have it all together not only told me I was OK, but I was special.

Needless to say, I was smitten. I made sure, however, to refer back to his girlfriend often so he understood that I understood he was with someone. I was very attracted to Ron, but I knew, like with straight friends I'd been attracted to in the past, that a boundary could never be crossed. I didn't expect any more from this relationship than making a great friend. It was as if I'd been released from prison after six years and I was seeing everything new for the first time. I was open to friendships with people who were not Christians. I wanted to learn from their perspectives. I was open to going wherever that may lead.

Ron didn't seem to want or need anything from me. His genuine concern was focused on me as a person and had nothing to do with my talent or abilities. As we talked, I let my guard down to let him see me as I was. "I'm divorced. I'm a failed ex-gay. I'm not sure if I'm gay or bi, or what's wrong with me. I'm just messed up in the head," I told Ron. He just smiled and took it all in stride.

For the next couple of months we'd get together and he'd help me work out. I started losing weight. I changed my diet and quit taking the medicine I'd been on for nearly 20 years. Ron was a wealth of information on physical health. I started seeing results pretty quickly and felt better than I had in a very long time.

Our friendship flourished, but so did our mutual attraction. I'd casually refused Ron's many advances, though it was becoming more difficult. We spent as much time as we could together, going to the gym, running, and eating out. Conversations about his girlfriend became less as we focused on our relationship. I had conveniently compartmentalized and minimized Ron's connection to her. The sexual tension between us intensified.

One afternoon we sat alone in my house. "I want to kiss you," he said. My heart raced. I'd never been more attracted to anyone than I was to Ron at that moment. This was different than anything I'd experienced up to this point. Like my research, I took a different perspective on this experience and removed the word "wrong" from it. The person in front of me was real and showed real interest in me, a fat, divorced, middle-aged man with so many imperfections.

"I'm afraid this will ruin everything," I said. "Your friendship is too valuable to me." I paused to include, "and you have a girlfriend" as an afterthought. Ron and I had talked about his sexual experiences in the past. As soon as there was sexual contact he became scared and cut off contact from the guys he'd been interested in. He was in love with his girlfriend, but he was inexplicably drawn to men. I didn't want to lose our relationship or become another casualty of Ron's fear.

"I'm not going anywhere," Ron said. "I've fallen in love with you." There was something in his eyes that made me believe him. It was something completely unexpected. I felt loved.

We never talked about love in ex-gay ministry, just sex. Love and homosexuality was a foreign concept. I thought the two were incompatible.

Ron knelt down in front of me, leaned forward and kissed me. My heart and resolve melted. Years of emotional, spiritual and psychological walls instantly dropped. My core, with all of its thoughts, emotions and feelings that lay dormant leapt to life. Deep within my existence something said, without any words, "This is what life is supposed to be. You were created to feel deeply and love deeply, without doubt, without shame, and without guilt."

Ron took me to my bedroom where the passion continued, uninhibited, and for the first time in my life I *made love* with someone. I was overwhelmed with a deep, emotional, and spiritual connection I'd never felt with another human being. It was the connection I'd longed for, to be known fully for who I was. It was as though someone turned the light on and I could see with absolute clarity.

Like stepping through the armoire into Narnia I discovered a world I didn't know existed. I *assumed*, standing around the kitchen table at 11 years old bantering with my friends, that having no feelings for a girl was normal. I *assumed* my friends felt the same sense of emptiness toward the opposite sex that I did. I thought life was perfunctory, going through the motions; making decisions about relationships was like deciding what kind of cereal to buy, and only absolute obedience to God's Word, as I understood it, brought peace and contentment. The Bible was the ultimate authority on relationships and living the American dream. So I thought.

This was none of that.

This feeling was euphoric. In an instant, romantic movies made sense; songs about relationships made sense. My love for God had been based on imagination, feelings, words in a book, and sermons from the pulpit. Ron was a real person, who embodied all of the things I couldn't have even dreamt about. His love was tangible, profound, and involved every one of my senses.

Homosexuality *wasn't* simply about sex, but about connection with people like me who were, for no explainable reason, attracted to the same gender. All of those years of ministry focused on the debauchery of homosexual sex were simply wrong. I never realized how deep of an intimate connection heterosexual couples could have because I could never experience that deep of a connection myself. All of that changed.

The next day I woke up after a completely restful night's sleep. I'm not sure how to describe the feeling I felt other than resolute. My body and mind felt at perfect peace. I was relaxed. No guilt. No remorse. This was very different than experiences I'd had in the past. I didn't feel the need to explain myself, question anything, or fix something.

The phone rang and it was Ron. "Hey," I said tenderly, "how are you feeling today?" I was concerned about the remorse Ron might have felt. At the same time, I knew it was a good sign that he called.

"I'm good," he said. "Like I told you yesterday, I'm not planning to go anywhere. I love you." I believed him. It felt good to be loved and to love someone back. Everything seemed to be falling into place for me. I'd managed to find the best of both worlds, being a dad of two biological kids and having a boyfriend who loved me. At the same time, in the back of my mind I knew there were complications in the relationship. He had a girlfriend, he was in the last few months of his doctoral program and he was moving back to Hawaii to start his practice. I was able to push all of that out of my mind for the time being. I'd justified our relationship as not cheating because I wasn't a girl. I didn't dwell on Ron's infidelity, or think about what this said about his character. In fact, I knew the struggle to hide one's sexual identity all too well. I understood him. I loved him the way he was. For a few sublime months, this kept me going.

The economy took a sudden downturn at the end of 2007 and I found myself unemployed. I didn't think too much about it, initially. I'd always been able to find work and corporate training paid well. Ron and I were seeing each other regularly. We'd text and talk on the phone, or stay at each other's places when time permitted and the kids weren't around. I continued losing weight, which added to my mental and physical health. Eventually, I found a temporary job, but I struggled to stay focused. All I could think about was Ron.

"I'm going home for the month of December," Ron told me. "School is on break and I'm going to spend time with my girlfriend." I knew this was coming, but was not prepared for it. My heart sunk. How was I going to live without Ron for an entire month? Besides,

I couldn't bear the thought of him with his girlfriend. They were probably going to have sex and I wondered if he'd be thinking of me. I now thought *she* was the problem between Ron and me.

I continued working at the company that hired me while Ron was gone, but the worries of what was going to happen to my relationship with Ron made it increasingly difficult to concentrate. I hated the work and struggled to keep my cool with the young team leader and her power trip. My communication with Ron grew increasingly distant. The anxiety that had been with me most of my life quickly stepped in to take his place. When my job suddenly ended and I was unable to find employment, my insecurities overwhelmed me.

Negative self talk, which I'd nurtured for years, once again told me that if I was really as lovable as Ron said, he wouldn't want to leave. I questioned whether the feelings I had were real, or just another figment of my imagination, like what I believed about God. I felt emotionally abandoned and in turn I began shutting my emotions off towards Ron. His emails to me while he was in Hawaii didn't make life any easier:

"Hi, Tim. I'd really forgotten how much I love Brenda. It's been really good being back home and reconnecting with her and the family. I can't keep cheating on her. I love you, but I also love her. I don't know where this leaves us. I have so much on my mind. I don't want to leave, but I can't wait to get back and talk to you."

Our communication sent me into a panic. The old tapes began playing in my head again: *You're really worthless. You don't have any value. Without him you're nothing.* Anxiety and depression quickly overcame me.

I called a friend and former co-worker of mine, with whom I'd spent countless hours witnessing to about Jesus. Ironically, she became a Christian in part because of my efforts. I came out to her about me and told her about my relationship with Ron. "You know he's cheating on her and you know you need to break it off," she said. I knew she was right. Besides, I knew Ron was leaving for his internship in three short months. I was paralyzed with fear.

Slowly, I allowed myself to think about my future. Ron wasn't in it. I wasn't moving to Hawaii and he wasn't staying in Sacramento. He planned to marry his girlfriend, who was completing her residency as a doctor in Oahu. They were young and in love. Ron wanted kids and I couldn't give that to him.

The more I thought about the future, the more devastated I became. I'd never felt love like that before. I didn't believe anyone would ever love me like that again. Ron was a fluke, I'd determined, and I was meant to be alone and unloved.

I was confused. I felt I'd been ushered into a new world of love, acceptance and possibilities and now I was being asked to leave. It was a human experience I'd always felt unworthy to receive, like a slap in the face from God that one of His greatest blessings of intimacy and connectedness was never meant for me.

In an emotional hurricane, I sent an email to Ron:

"I think it's best if we don't communicate anymore. I'm deleting this email account. I wish you and Brenda all the best. I love you."

My heart was broken. Ron called repeatedly in spite of my refusal to talk with him. His persistence was enough to make me answer my phone after a couple of weeks. "I can't do this, Ron," I said as my voice trembled. I was leaving the grocery store and barely made it out without breaking down in front of the clerk. "I miss you so much and I don't want to go back to life before you. It hurts too much."

"I miss you, too," he reassured me. He sounded confident and his voice soothed me. "I'm sorry. I didn't mean to hurt you. I'm just really confused. I don't want to lose Brenda, but I don't want to lose you either." My self-protections melted and I broke down sobbing.

"I don't know what to do," I said.

"I think you should see other people," he countered.

"Doesn't that bother you?" I asked, hoping he'd recant his statement.

"It bothers me a lot, but the only experience you have with relationships with anyone is with me. I think it would be good for you to see if you really love me."

"I don't know if I could see other people." I said. "I feel like I'd be cheating on you." I'd always been a one-person dater. Two years after my divorce I tried dating a woman but couldn't get past the feeling that I was still married and cheating on my wife. I hated my wife, but still felt guilty. I couldn't imagine what it would be like to do that to someone I really loved.

"I love you, Tim, but I plan to marry Brenda. I would feel better if I knew you were with someone who cared about you the way that I do."

On New Year's Eve I put up another Craigslist ad to find someone to be with. My heart was still with Ron, but he was in Hawaii with Brenda and I had to figure out a way to move forward. Paul responded to my ad. It was my first blind date, of sorts. We went to dinner and watched a movie. Paul told me about some of his sexual escapades. I listened with interest. I'd never been involved in anything like that because sex outside of marriage was not an option for me as a Christian. Paul, like me, was a divorced father. His son was around the same age of one of my girls. I thought Paul and I could be good friends.

"Do you mind if I kiss you?" he asked as we sat on the couch in his home. I wasn't expecting that. I thought of Ron and remembered that he said it was a good idea for me to experiment with other people. This seemed to be an opportune time to let go and see what would happen. Paul and I kissed and before I knew it, we ended up in his bedroom.

Unlike my experience with Ron, the next day was filled with regret. Paul was a nice guy, but it was quickly evident that his lifestyle was not like mine. I wasn't into sexual escapades and orgies. This was the first time I'd ever had a one-night stand. It didn't make me feel good. In fact, I felt rather used and I was embarrassed by what I had done. Paul and I emailed a couple of times, but the contact stopped rather quickly when he started talking about the person he was in love with, and it wasn't me.

I sheepishly shared my experience with my ex-wife. She didn't judge me. Instead, she compassionately listened. "Yeah, it doesn't feel good to be used," she said. "You can only pick up and go on." We had reached a completely different place in our relationship. Honestly, I felt like I'd sunk to her level. At the same time, my heart toward her and her experiences softened. Maybe I'd judged her too harshly. I wasn't quite ready to lay down my moral sword, but I began seeing her, and others, differently. Sexual experiences outside of marriage didn't lessen one's value or make that person less human. In fact, in some ways, they became more human. Sexuality meets a basic need for intimacy and connection. I understood that now.

A few days later Ron called. "I'll be there on Saturday. Can you pick me up at the airport? We can talk more."

I paused for a moment, thinking of all the pain I'd experienced over the last month and of the experience I'd just had with Paul. "Sure," I said, allowing my heart to feel his warm embrace. I needed to see him, if only one more time.

Ron arrived late on Saturday evening and I decided to take him to my house so he could sleep. His apartment was another 40 minutes away. We climbed into bed, both of us emotionally tired, and Ron physically tired from his long flight. His mind raced with thoughts of his girlfriend back home, while mine raced with thoughts of Ron. He was distant, yet tried to engage with me. We embraced each other, but it wasn't like before. The night slowly turned sexual, but lacked the emotional intimacy I'd felt previously. I was content for the moment to at least hold him again. I was acutely aware that our relationship had changed, and was coming to an end. I felt my heart breaking.

Ron and I continued the discussions over the next month, but it was I who finally found the intestinal fortitude to tell Ron I couldn't see him anymore. It was just a few weeks before he was leaving for his residency in Nashville, and then graduating two months later. I felt empty, but decided, like so many times before, to stuff my feelings and go at it alone.

Bailouts were in full swing at this point and no one was hiring. In addition to the emotional strife I felt over losing the one person I ever truly loved, my financial stability crumbled. The Employment Development Department wasn't sending unemployment checks and I couldn't reach anyone to find out why. I couldn't pay my mortgage and I couldn't find work. I was on a financially sinking ship and there was nothing I could do about it. I was literally on the verge of bankruptcy for the first time in my life. Fortunately, my ex-wife kept the lights on and put food on the table.

I was on a different journey now. I felt confident that my kids were taken care of and it was time to figure out who I was. In a strange way, it felt like I'd entered puberty for the first time. Like a teenage boy, I was full of testosterone, trying to navigate my way around relationships. With Ron out of my life I needed someone to make me feel better about being me, especially in light of my inability to financially care for my own family.

My hope of finding love had deteriorated, but my sexual appetite was alive. I didn't realize how I had repressed and neglected my sexuality as a teenager. There was no outlet…until now. For better or worse, I was old enough to date whom I wanted and do what I wanted. The song "Looking for Love in all the Wrong Places" didn't make more sense to me than it did in this period of my life.

If I didn't already feel like I wasn't good enough as a human being, I discovered how much the mainstream gay community focused on looks and youth. Ron had given me enough confidence in my looks by his many compliments and helped me achieve the body of my dreams. I'd dropped fifty pounds, actually having to put a little weight back on to normalize. I was fit, looking younger than my age, and discovered that others found me sexually desirable. I compensated for my insecurities by going to the gym five days a week, though it didn't change how I felt about my own self-worth. I still needed someone to tell me, or show me, that I was worth loving.

My online life became all-consuming. Ron had unlocked a door of passion. Posting and answering ads on Craigslist was like playing the lottery. I desperately wanted to be loved and believed that the next connection was going to be *the one*. At first, I was picky, looking for men who acted like straight men, lived in the suburbs and didn't do drugs or drink. I really didn't want to just hook up; I wanted to go on dates, fall in love and have my Hollywood ending.

As time went by I became more desperate. My self-worth hung on every response, email and meeting. Positive responses validated me, but meeting someone who didn't request a second date implied I wasn't attractive enough, or the right type. I checked my email constantly and lived on an emotional roller coaster, trying to gain someone's attention. Frequently, I laid on my bed and cried, wanting all this pain to end, losing hope that I'd ever find my true love. I constantly questioned what my experience with Ron was all about. At the same time I couldn't get him out of my mind. A popular country song on the radio at the time became the anthem for my time with Ron.

> *I never knew 'til you were gone*
> *How many pages you were on*
> *It never ends I keep turning*
> *And line after line and you are there again*
> *I don't know how to let you go*
> *You are so deep down in my soul*
> *I feel helpless so hopeless*
> *It's a door that never closes*
> *No I don't know how to do this*

[Chorus]

I've talked to friends
I've talked to myself
I've talked to God
I prayed liked hell but I still miss you
I tried sober I tried drinking
I've been strong and I've been weak
And I still miss you
I've done everything to
Move on like I'm supposed to
I'd give anything for one more minute with you
I still miss you.

(Anderson, Sellers, Nichols, 2008)

Love songs, which were once benign and meaningless, were now too painful to listen to. I was once able to stuff and repress feelings, but that was no longer working. I knew too much. I'd felt too much.

I placed ads for both men and women when I decided to hit the dating scene, but it soon became apparent that dating a woman meant going back into the closet and hiding a part of me that had taken a long time to come to terms with. I wasn't willing to do that.

My desire for love and my affinity for sex now went hand in hand. I ultimately pictured myself settling down in my suburban home, raising my kids and being in love. Over the next two years I dated, had encounters and one-night stands with a number of men.

I discovered a popular hook up site, which touts its ability to allow people to hook up any time with anyone for sex.

The thought of having sex with some of the people I saw on the site was quite appealing, not to mention the rush of having sex with multiple partners. But the analytical side of me wondered who these people were and why they would do this? Are they perverts, horny, or is there something more to this? Perhaps they were, like me, just looking for love. I signed up.

My first meeting was with a man named Rico. We met in a downtown Sacramento restaurant. My fear of what negative thing could happen, like being kidnapped or murdered, overwhelmed my compulsion for a sexual encounter. "Hi, Rico," I said as we sat down at a small table off to the side of the room. We exchanged cordial greetings. "Can I ask you a question?"

Rico didn't seem very comfortable, but said, "Sure."

"Why are you doing this?"

"I'm married," he said, "and things haven't been going very well in my marriage. I think she's cheating on me. Neither one of us is happy."

"Have you talked about your marriage with your wife?" I asked.

"No, not really." Rico looked down and drifted into thought.

"What do you get out of this?" I probed, shifting into therapist mode.

"I think it's just a stress reliever. I feel stuck and I don't see a way out of my situation."

"Interesting," I said. "I wonder if your wife feels the same. Do you worry about contracting an STD and bringing that home to your wife?"

"We don't really have sex much anymore," Rico confided. "I don't know. This isn't really what I want. Honestly, I haven't had sex with anyone. We just seem to meet and talk and leave." That was about to happen again.

Rico and I talked for the next hour, deciding that we weren't going to hook up either. I felt compassion for him and wanted to help him with his marriage. I think that compassion was what led me into the ministry in the first place. "It was nice meeting you," I said as we got up to leave. "I really hope you find what you're looking for and things work out for you."

Rico's eyes locked with mine. "Thanks, man. You, too."

I walked back to my car feeling like I'd made a difference in someone's life. It wasn't necessarily what I signed up for, but at the same time I'd made a human connection and that's really what I wanted.

Others I met over the phone, through email and online chat. I asked similar questions and, surprisingly, discovered the depth of what they were looking for was much more than a quick hookup. People came from all walks of life and had different reasons for why they wanted an encounter with a stranger.

Clyde looked hot in his picture. He was a bicycle rider and posed provocatively in his bicycle shorts. *Perhaps*, I thought, *this will be the guy.* We met at a local pizza joint in the gay district of Sacramento. At this point I'd developed a list of interview questions for the people I'd been meeting from the sex site.

"So, what brings you here, Clyde?" I asked with the confidence I'd gained over the last few weeks. He didn't look much like his picture.

"You brought me here," he said with a seductive smile.

Gross, I thought. "Why do you meet strangers online for sex?"

"I've met a lot of hot guys and I really like sex," Clyde answered. Like so many others I'd interviewed I knew there had to be more to his story, but his effeminate mannerisms and overt come-ons were turning my stomach. He was someone I knew I didn't want to be with. After sharing a pizza and struggling through a conversation to find common ground, or to even find mental stimulation, I wanted to leave.

"So, you want to go back to my place?" he asked. He seemed to not notice any of the social cues that said I wanted nothing to do with him.

"No, I don't think this will work out," I said. He made a pouty face.

"Well, OK, but if you change your mind you have my number."

I went home that night and cancelled my membership to the site. My curiosity as to why so many people looked for hook-ups was satisfied for the time being.

I knew I was driven to find love and acceptance, but I didn't make the connection between my behavior and my need. However, I saw it clearly in the lives of the men I met. I was divorced. I didn't have to hide anything and no longer had someone to hide it from. That wasn't exactly true. I still hadn't told most of the significant people in my life, nor had I completely accepted that this would be my fate. I did, however, find acceptance from my ex-wife.

In fact, she accepted my homosexuality long before I did. She had determined early on that I was gay, in spite of my ex-gay profession. She decided that she wasn't willing to live a life with someone where there was a wall that kept us from experiencing complete intimacy. She endured judgment from family and pastors for her decision to end the marriage. Our family pastor told her it would be seven years before I would really begin to deal with my issues. Strangely, he was exactly right. Seven years later, I was beginning to come to terms with my sexuality. She had a front row seat to the transformation. I felt the freedom to experience this new life, especially with the mother of my kids on my side.

Frustrated with the seedier side of online personals, I met Todd through a more conventional dating website. He was a flight attendant. I found him very attractive. Like me, he was divorced and had two kids, slightly younger than mine. We met at his townhome after talking online for a couple of weeks. He was equally attracted to me and when the sexual tension became too strong, we gave in to our temptation. The passion was intense. When it was over, however, Todd looked at me and said, "OK, you can leave now." He laughed, but the look in his eyes told me he wasn't kidding. I laughed with him. Gradually, I gathered my things and left his house a little after midnight.

The next day I sent Todd a text, but his response wasn't nearly as fast as it had been prior to our encounter. I justified his statement about leaving after sex to his just being tired. Besides, Todd did text me back and told me he had to leave town early the next day. He wasn't able to text until later.

I was proud of the fact that I'd found someone as attractive as Todd, who, I thought, shared my family values and who found me equally attractive. I made mental plans for bringing our kids together. Like most encounters, when I was with someone my mental state was good and that translated into my relationships with my kids and the people around me. I was still unemployed during this time, trying to negotiate with the bank to save my house. I needed this relationship. Todd and I got together a couple more times over the next month. In between our rendezvous he was always slow to respond back to me and always had an excuse why.

I began to wonder if Todd was seeing anyone else. He never answered my questions directly. I wanted him to like me as much as I liked him, and as long as he eventually responded to my emails and texts – and I sent a lot of them – I was OK to stay in my fantasy world that we would be together.

One day Todd called me and said, "Tim, this isn't going to work out."

"Why not?" I asked. "You said you were looking for someone to settle down with and so am I."

"Well, I was wrong. This just isn't the right time and I'm busy. I'm really sorry."

I hung up the phone feeling stupid. I should have known. He got what he wanted out of me. *Once again, I'm a nobody*, I thought. The self-esteem and value I got out of the relationships went as quickly as it came. I felt like I kept giving pieces of me away and coming back with less than I had before.

I'd like to think I'm a quick learner. While that may be true in some areas, when it came to relationships, my emotional ability to distinguish truth from fiction was nearly nonexistent. This part of my life lasted for almost two years. In hindsight, I prostituted myself to find value. I let others determine my self-worth time and time again. I looked for a sense of belonging that constantly eluded me. I knew I was gay, and was trying to accept that I was gay, but I still didn't fit anywhere. No one wanted me. I thought it was because I wasn't good enough, attractive enough, or smart enough.

By the summer of 2008, I'd landed a more permanent contract position in San Jose, California, where I stayed during the week. I was able to put my finances back in order and decided it was time to make some better decisions about my life. In the back of my mind I always thought about what my life must look like to my kids. I wanted to be an example for them, but made excuses for why I wasn't acting like I should. I came to the decision that love was elusive. If I couldn't have love then I needed to have friends.

I looked up the San Jose Lesbian, Gay, Bisexual and Transgender Center and decided to attend a meeting. I had never set foot in such a building and couldn't escape the ingrained thought that I was "entering the enemy's camp." I arrived a few minutes early and saw the rainbow flag flying over the parking lot. No one knew me in San Jose, but I checked over my shoulders to make sure I didn't see anyone who might recognize me from the company for which I was consulting. I noticed several places where the building was in need of repair as I made my way through the corridor. An older woman, who appeared straight, sat at the receptionist's desk down the hallway from the entrance and directed me to the room where the meeting was held.

"Welcome!" a middle-aged white man bellowed as I walked in. I'm sure I looked as scared as I felt. "We're going to wait a few more minutes and see who else shows up," he said. He opened a sandwich he'd picked up on the way to the meeting. "I hope you don't mind if I eat while we're waiting. I came right over here after work."

I politely smiled. "No problem. Go right ahead."

Two more people showed up a few minutes later. One was a husky-looking basketball player in his mid-twenties. He came from the local college. The other was an effeminate black kid, who looked no more than 18 or 19 years old.

"Welcome, everyone. My name is George and this group is for people who are just coming out or want to learn more about coming out as LGBT." George was rather abrupt, like a football coach. He dramatically told his coming out story. He was married to a woman and working at a nice job when he decided he didn't want to hide his sexuality. So he announced to his family, all at once, his intention to divorce his wife and marry his lover. His story had all the elements of a Jerry Springer episode, complete with name-calling and back-stabbing the people he supposedly loved. "Who's next?" George asked, glancing rapidly at the three of us around the table.

I was too stunned to speak. Drama really wasn't my thing and I couldn't help but judge George and some of his actions. *You're not in church anymore*, I thought.

"Well, I'll go next," whispered the black kid. "My name is Demetrius and I was raised in church. My dad is a pastor." I'd seen a lot of people like Demetrius. I played keyboards in black churches for years and learned about the "brothers on the down low" or the "DL," as it was called. It was an interesting phenomenon to me as a white person. In my circles there were "Christians" and then there were "black Christians." Black Christians were the ones who went to church on Sundays, shouted, sang, danced or even played in the band and sang in the choir, but lived like God didn't exist when they weren't in church. They weren't *real* Christians.

This kid reminded me of an organist named Jamar I worked with when I played for a black choir in Sacramento. Jamar's sexual identity was so flamboyant it came into the room before he did. Yet, no one in the choir ever talked about it. When playing at a service one night with the choir, the pastor got up to take an offering. "If we don't support these young people," he preached, "they'll end up playing in bars and dance clubs instead of playing for God where they belong." I was fairly certain Jamar spent plenty of time in bars and dance clubs and was a little baffled as to how no one else could see that.

"No one knows I'm gay," Demetrius continued, "except for my dad." I mentally rolled my eyes. *Everyone knows you're gay, dude!* I thought. Clearly, he was clueless about how effeminate he was. Demetrius went on to share his story of rejection by his mother and the embarrassment his homosexuality would cause the congregation if they knew. Interestingly, he said his dad was OK with it and encouraged him to be who he was. Demetrius seemed to have a lot on his mind and a lot more to get off his chest. He talked for a long time.

The last guy briefly shared that as a basketball player he didn't feel he could come out because his teammates would tease him. He didn't have much more to say. He didn't look gay at all. For the longest time I wondered if he was in the wrong place. I could relate to him, though. I didn't look gay either and always felt guarded because I didn't want anyone to find out about me.

"What about you?" George looked directly at me.

"It's a long story," I said half-smiling. "I'm out, I guess, I'm just not sure where to go from here." Demetrius seemed lost in his own world of thought. The basketball player looked down and George was finishing up his chips. No one seemed that interested in what I had to say. As a speaker I'd learned to read the crowd and when they lose interest it's time to quit talking. "But that's cool," I continued. "I'm just checking things out."

I really wanted someone to ask me a question, show concern and draw me out, but it was late. I was uncomfortable there. I didn't really find anyone I thought might be a friend. George concluded the meeting and I slipped out the door without talking to anyone else.

The ride back to my rented room was filled with much thought. I was lonely. I'd gone too far away from my Christian foundation to go back and, besides, I'd learned too much to really believe it anymore. The road ahead of me was daunting and filled with uncertainty. It was evident that I didn't fit in the mainstream gay community. Then again, I was still a registered Republican. I knew that wouldn't go over well.

Making new friends was hard enough, but now I felt thrust into a world of people who really weren't like me, other than our shared sexual orientation. In my old life I felt I had to hide the fact I was gay. In my new life I had to hide the fact that I was once ex-gay and involved in the Evangelical Church. Leaving the Church didn't make the shame go away, it just moved it from one lie to another.

After a stint in the Bay Area I was able to come back home full time to Sacramento. I had heard of Meetup.com, a social website where people with shared interests could meet in public group settings. I found a gay professional group and decided to give it a try.

I sat across the table from Michael and Manuel at my first-ever gay Meetup. Jack, who recently moved into the Sacramento area from Atlanta, Georgia, had just started the Meetup. His Southern charm put me at ease. Our shared experience of the South gave me something to talk about with him. I falsely assumed that Jack was more conservative than the gay people in California.

It was 2008 and the town of Sacramento was abuzz with Proposition 8, the now infamous proposition to overturn the ban on gay marriage.

"Did any of you have a chance to help out at the Gay and Lesbian Center on Prop 8?" asked Jack.

Michael put down his fork and politely wiped his mouth, "I went there as often as I could," he said. Manuel nodded in agreement. The conversation continued for a few minutes about the evils of Prop 8 and who was behind it. My stomach turned. I had nothing to add to the conversation. In fact, I had voted yes on Proposition 8. It wasn't about gay marriage for me it was about the ability of a judge to overturn the vote of the people that was of most concern.

I managed to dodge the question altogether, but meeting these people didn't exactly help me find my "peeps." If ever there was diversity, it was me: a gay, American-Indian, conservative, who sang black-gospel music.

Dinner was soon over and as we got up to leave Jack said, "Before we go, let's get a picture."

I wasn't sure how to gracefully decline so I smiled and said, "Sure! Why not?!" I knew why not. I occasionally substitute taught at my kids' Christian school. If they found out I was gay, I would never be able to teach there again. I contacted Jack that night after I got home and asked that he not post my picture on the website. Graciously, he agreed. It would be another year before I came back again.

Anderson, Keith, Sellers, Jason, Nichols, Tim, I still Miss You, Columbia Records, 2008

– 8 –
GIVING UP

I WAS FULLY ENGAGED in my master's program during the fall of 2008. In hindsight, school was exactly what I needed to get my life back on track. I was still in the midst of hookups and searching for someone to love me, but school gave me a mental focus.

I believed that homosexuality was abnormal, but "it is what it is," I'd decided and I was going to make the best of it. I was tired of feeling like there was something wrong with me. My belief that it was a learned behavior had faded as I read different studies and theories on what makes people gay. Still, studying education, about how humans learn and what influences the way we perceive what we learn, appealed to me.

Next to so many of my cohorts, I felt unqualified to be there. Many of these people were education professionals, had multiple degrees and were focused. I didn't feel I measured up to them in any way, having stumbled into corporate education. I brought more questions than experience.

I decided that emotions were counterintuitive to my success and truth could only be found in the data. As evidence I thought back to years of growing up in the Pentecostal church. I couldn't even count how many "healing" services I'd sat through, played in, and sang for, which ultimately led to no physical or permanent emotional changes in people at all. People with cancer still had cancer, and most died; colds and flus still lasted the usual 7-10 days; and divorces still went forward, including my own.

I'd taken an interest in neuroscience and began listening to lectures and reading articles on neuropsychology. I saw just how tied our emotions are to our biology and how our personalities are connected to our heredity. I learned how changes to our brains affect our emotions and learned about the limbic system, from which emotions emanate. Emotions are biological responses to the stimuli around us. They can make us believe things to be true, because we *feel* that they are. I had learned to distrust belief; I had learned to distrust my own feelings.

I became especially interested in transformative learning, which is a perspective change usually brought on by some sort of cognitive dissonance. Social psychologist Leon Festinger described cognitive dissonance as an incongruent relationship between thoughts and our understanding of those thoughts, resulting in excessive mental stress and discomfort (1957). I'd experienced transformative learning firsthand, trying to resolve the conflict over my sexual orientation and divorce in light of my understanding of God and the Bible. I changed what I believed because my beliefs simply didn't match my reality. No matter how much I *wished* my beliefs were true, they simply were not.

Now, my beliefs were suspended. I wasn't ready to call myself an atheist because that would mean the matter was settled. Nothing was settled. The only thing I knew for certain was that I existed.

How I got here and how I got to be the way I was, was yet to be discovered.

Boiling below my conscious thought was intense anger. Like a jilted ex-husband, I held resentment. I felt duped. I felt lied to. None of my expectations were met when it came to what I believed or thought about God. I'd wondered where He was when I made the decision to get married. Where was God through all of those years of trying to change my sexual orientation? I believed He loved me and wanted the best for me, but that didn't seem to be the case during those years of torment. Nature took its course without interruption. People made decisions in spite of my prayers. My children were growing up in two homes despite my willingness to stay in the closet and lie about who I really was. If there were a God, He took sadistic delight in my inability to succeed.

Yet, I didn't know at what, or whom, I should be angry. Ex-gay ministry? Organized religion? It would have been easier to deal with my anger if it came with a face. Instead, it was a belief, a philosophy, a set of values, and an ideal. I put my faith in something that took the shape of a wish and what I presumed to be absolute truth. The thing that I believed was gone, but the resentment and anger toward it remained.

For the next few years the topic of religion, Christianity in particular, remained off limits to friends and family. Anger simmered beneath what I thought was a stoic exterior, though I argued that I had moved on. I comfortably distanced myself from my kids' Bible assignments in their Christian school, cordially interacted with their teachers and judged the administration for their intolerance of others.

Anger, I discovered, was a really good way to keep from feeling other emotions and lent itself well in my quest for intellectual answers. I maintained my good-natured humor, but didn't see the impact of anger on my inability to find intimacy.

Welling up inside of me was the need to fully come out. I'd moved from one secret life to another, meeting men, some of them married, who hid behind their sexual exploits in an attempt to satisfy their need to be intimately known. The encounters weren't working for me. I couldn't explain the feeling inside. Perhaps it was simply years of psychological repression, or like a physical symptom showing a chronic disease, it was letting me know it needed to be healed. The torment of hiding was too much.

At the same time, I was embarrassed to be associated with gay people. The term "gay" had a negative connotation, even to me. I wasn't like *those* people. I looked and acted like a straight man. I had kids. I didn't drink, or go to bars. My political beliefs were more in line with Evangelicals than gays. My concept of homosexuality came from years of living on the right side of politics and religion: all gay men are effeminate, like to dress in drag, are promiscuous and have no moral compass. They are atheists, political activists and out to destroy the very fabric of society. I knew from my brief stint in the gay community that my perceptions were sweeping generalizations and stereotypes, but years of indoctrination colored those perceptions of what it meant to be gay.

My ex-wife's family was the first to know since they were so involved with our lives and our children's lives. I had grown distant from my own parents because I was afraid they would reject me if they knew who I had become. When my sister came to visit I finally built up the courage to tell her. She already knew about my involvement with ex-gay ministry and even told me when I entered, "If that's what you want to do I'll support you, but whether you're gay or not doesn't matter to me."

In many ways, I felt responsible for my sister's Christian conversion. I thought by showing her that Christianity worked (i.e., God healed my homosexuality and gave me a successful marriage), she and her husband would ultimately come to Jesus. My parents and I prayed for her and her family. Coming out to her was an admission of failure more than anything, but I was in a different place. I'd come to believe that maybe she was right and that the God our family believed in didn't exist after all.

"I'm gay," I blurted as we drove up to my parent's house. She was visiting from Virginia where she lived. We were coming back from the store to make a family dinner.

"Oh, OK," she said. "I was kind of wondering what was going on with you, but didn't really want to ask."

"I didn't think you'd care," I said, "but I felt the need to be honest about where I am in life."

"Look, I'll tell you what I told my daughter, 'I don't care if you're gay or straight, just don't tell me you're a Democrat.'" She laughed.

"I need to think of a way to tell Mom and Dad," I said.

"Don't do that. He's old. I don't think he would ever understand. Just let him die in peace," she said with concern. I love my sister and respect her beyond words, but I needed to tell them for my own peace of mind.

It's difficult to explain what was going on in the core of my being. I can only describe it as an internal tsunami; an earthquake shaking the floor of my center, which caused a force so strong that my truth could no longer be contained. If I didn't come out, and come out specifically to my parents, I was going to have a nervous breakdown. Perhaps what I experienced is really nothing more than the human condition to be known for who we are so that we can be loved for who we are.

I lived for my parents' approval, even in my forties. I wasn't exactly sure how I got there or why it mattered to me, but it did. I was embarrassed by the thought of them thinking I was having gay sex and what that even meant. I knew they were concerned about my salvation as it was. I'd changed through the years and stopped talking about God or the Bible. As my dad always said, "You can tell a lot about someone's relationship with God by how they respond when the topic comes up." I changed the subject.

Christians prayed earnestly for people like me. I know; I was on the other side for decades. I was in the circles that worried and prayed about those who strayed away from the gospel and into a life of sin. I'd wondered how it was even possible, especially after having been so involved in church for so many years. Now here I was. I knew exactly what it felt like. I didn't feel I belonged on either side.

What does a person do who spends 25 years of his life as a minister and then suddenly doesn't believe it anymore? I floundered. I searched for purpose and meaning, while trying to avoid the people in my past who could possibly help me find it. The more pressing issue was simply coming to terms with a sexual orientation that never fit into a belief system, which guided nearly every aspect of my life.

By the beginning of 2009 sexual promiscuity had gotten old. I was tired of meeting people who never talked to me again. I was tired of starting relationships over and over. It took a long time for me to get to know people and feel comfortable. I was desperate to integrate that one man into my life and introduce him to my world, but only occasionally did we get to the point that someone met my kids before he moved on, or the relationship fizzled. I'd given up on romantic relationships. I figured that the best romantic relationship would be based on friendship first anyway, and I decided to try another Meetup.com group.

I made a new friend online who, at our very first meeting said, "I like you, but I'm not the least bit interested in having a relationship with you." I thought he was attractive, but concurred. Joseph was more like me, in that he looked and acted like a straight guy. He worked in construction for several years before he was laid off. He was also in the process of coming out and this was all new for him. We hit the gay scene together to offer each other support and meet other people.

One night we decided to go to the local gay bar. It was a dark place on the corner of a busy street in the gay district of downtown Sacramento. I was definitely one of the older people there. Music videos played above our heads on a string of monitors scattered throughout the room. Joseph arrived shortly after I got there and we hugged like we were old friends.

Hugging people you've just met in the gay community is the norm. It's the simple gesture that says, "I understand you. I understand the difficult journey you've been on and want you to know that you're not alone." In spite of the various backgrounds, social statuses, ages and experiences, a certain camaraderie exists among gay people, which I had not found in the straight community.

I ordered a bottle of water and sat at the bar with Joseph. We exchanged war stories of the pain we had gone through, as well as where we were in the coming out process. At the same time we people-watched and pointed at guys one or both of us found attractive.

I could barely hear Joseph above the blaring music. I just didn't see myself fitting into that scene. Yet, after years of obeying the rules I was spreading my wings. I wouldn't have been caught dead in a bar when I was a teenager or in my early twenties. In fact, it never really appealed to me. Now, with God removed from the picture, all bets were off. I was ready to explore places I'd never been before.

Joseph and I made our way into the gay community together. If one of us heard of a Meetup group happening, he'd invite the other one. We'd give each other moral support and courage to make friends. I soon realized that Joseph was interested in a different kind of person than me.

Simon caught Joseph's eye at a local pub where we were meeting. At first I thought Joseph was kidding. Simon embodied all of the gay stereotypes that movies portray and reality TV adores. If I thought I'd conquered my own homophobia, Simon was about to reveal the raging Evangelical Republican that dwelt inside.

"Hey, cutie," he said to Joseph while clutching his gold lamé coin purse.

"Hi." Joseph smiled. I was watching what looked like a bad b-movie unfolding in front of my eyes.

"My friends and I are going to a bar down the street to hang out some more. Do you want to come with us?" Simon asked. I was certain Joseph would say no.

"Yeah, sure. Why not?" he said and looked at me, "You wanna go?" Simon disgusted me. I wasn't sure what this half-man-mostly-girl was up to, but my suspicions ran high. I reluctantly went with Joseph and his new friends to the bar, mostly because I felt Joseph was going to need an alibi.

Simon carried most of the conversation, waving his thin little arms around like a junior high girl, sauntering back and forth to the bar to refill his drink. My disgust must have been written all over my face. I answered his occasional questions, though he was mostly interested in talking about himself and flirting with Joseph.

"I don't like you," he eventually said to me with a dead stare as we all sat around the small table. His friends laughed nervously.

"It's OK," I said, "I don't like you either." More nervous laughter followed.

I'd spent an enormous amount of my life working to find status, earn money, degrees, and respect. Simon and his friends, all much younger than I, looked like they rolled out of bed and expected to be rewarded. They didn't want to play by the rules; they just wanted the benefits of the hard work. I don't think I realized how much their entitlement to acceptance – just because they were there – bothered me. After a few more minutes, I decided it was time to leave and that Joseph could take care of himself.

I walked back to my car trying to make sense of Joseph's poor choice. More than that, I was rattled from coming face-to-face with the very thing I despised: men who acted like women. *It's not right*, I thought. *If I wanted a girl I'd date one. If a guy is gay why would he be interested in someone so effeminate?* I was confused and definitely out of my comfort zone. Unlike my first run-in with the gay community, I didn't retreat so quickly into my corner. Meeting Joseph encouraged me to see that there were others out there like me, minus the inexplicable attraction to girls in men's bodies.

Jack created a gay singles Meetup group and I decided to see what was there. Joseph, now rid of the atrocity that plagued him for over a month, was supposed to meet me there but, for some reason, I ended up going alone.

The dress code for these Meetups encouraged attendees to step it up and represent a community that embodied fashion and style. I only owned two pairs of shoes, three if you counted the ones I used to mow the lawn. My casual shoes were white New Balance sneakers. I'm color-blind and can't even identify some of the shades of paint on my walls at home. My sense of fashion is so poor that at one point I put on a pair of jeans when the weather began to cool, after wearing shorts all summer, and my daughter asked if I had a job interview. Needless to say, my interaction with the gay community left me feeling a little self-conscious.

I was one of the first to arrive at Jack's singles' group. The bar was more upscale than the one I went to downtown and we had a room off to the side. I ordered my obligatory bottle of water and scanned the room. The group included mostly older men who were well-educated and offered stimulating conversation, but, quite frankly, lacked personality. It seemed another glaring difference between the gay community and me. I love education, science, and discussions on the deeper issues of life, but my lowbrow sense of humor is never far from reach. It was fine, I reasoned. Most of these men were close to retirement age. My life was just starting.

I pulled up a chair between two conversations and listened to both. My ears perked up when I heard someone introduce himself as the Dean of the Sociology Department at a local college.

"Oh, that's cool!" a younger guy chimed in. "I'm a psychology major." I moved my chair into the conversation.

"Hi, I'm Tim," I said, uncharacteristically butting into the conversation. "I'm an education major who studies brain-learning."

"I'm Abel," said the younger guy.

"I'm Frederick," the sociology professor inserted. His disinterest in the conversation was evident, but that didn't stop me from asking my usual get-to-know-you questions: Why do you do what you do? How did you get interested in your field? Why do you like doing your job? Abel, on the other hand, took an immediate interest and it wasn't long before our conversation excluded Professor Why-are you-bothering-me and we focused on each other.

Beside Abel's propensity for the intellectual, he also had a quick wit, had gone through ex-gay ministry and was in the process of coming to terms with his Christian beliefs and his sexual orientation. Had I not met him at the singles' group, I would never have guessed he was gay.

Over the next few months, I made relationships with a number of people away from the bar scene. Some invited me into their homes where we shared stories of our family lives and what coming out was like for each of us. A theme of shame, sadness and heartbreak was common. One friend, Juan, born in Puerto Rico also grew up in a Pentecostal home. He shared the experience of being thrown out of his house because of a sexual identity he couldn't change. Somewhere he found the fortitude to say, "I've learned not to put energy into people who don't accept me the way I am."

I realized I was still very concerned with what people would think of me if I came out. I didn't realize I projected my own thoughts of me on others and presumed they would think the worst. It was ironic really. I'd spent my entire life cutting off relationships because of shame and I was simultaneously afraid of losing relationships I had a history of cutting off.

Embracing homosexuality and all of its nuances – including people like Simon – was a long way off. I didn't want to be associated with effeminate men. Coming out with abandon left me vulnerable to the worst thoughts of others. I'd spent too much time sculpting what others thought of me to simply let go.

I sat across the table from Abel at a local hamburger joint at the downtown mall. "I swear I invited Joseph and Michael and I thought they were coming," I told him. This was the second or third time I made plans for my friends to get together and it ended up just being Abel and me. I was embarrassed that he thought I was setting him up and trying to get him alone.

"Yeah, right!" he said, laughing. "It is rather suspicious that you keep *inviting people*," he emphasized with air quotes, "but they never seem to get the message."

Abel was not like anyone else I'd met. Ever. I wouldn't classify him as 'my type,' per se. Although I was attracted to his boyish good looks, he is significantly younger than me, is an awkward body type, didn't have the education that was on my "must have" list and identified himself as a gay Christian. This was particularly awkward since I had decidedly distanced myself from religion. Yet, the more time we spent together the more I found myself drawn to him.

His extroverted personality is the opposite of mine. He's unimpressed with degrees or education. His generosity, particularly to those who are less fortunate, is without any expectation or strings attached. In fact, his response to someone who uses something of his is, "Oh, good! I'm glad you got some benefit out of it." And he means it. His wisdom and life experience goes well beyond his years and his selfless love is something of which Hollywood movies are made.

"How does someone ask you out?" I asked him one night months after we met.

"Oh, I don't know. How does someone ask you out?" He wasn't taking the hint.

"I'm trying to ask you to go out with me," I blurted. (His version of the story adds "idiot" on the end of that sentence.)

"Oh." Obviously, he was taken aback, but apparently flattered. "Well, I guess like that," he said.

Dating Abel added a new dimension to our relationship. True to his nature he was "all in" right from the beginning. I was hesitant and apprehensive about getting into a relationship at that point. I'd been hurt repeatedly and feared I'd opened a door that would eventually be slammed in my face.

I didn't pay much attention to Abel's confession of faith as a gay Christian. We'd talked about it a few times but I simply couldn't wrap my brain around the idea that someone could be gay and Christian. Unlike me, Abel was not raised in church. His affiliation was Presbyterian, which, according my former beliefs, didn't have much to do with Christianity anyway. Besides, I didn't see how his faith made any difference to the way he lived. That said, he is much more conservative than me when it comes to morality and his stance on issues regarding abortion and politics.

My relationship with Abel brought the stability to my life that had been lacking. Surfing the web for online relationships ended and I'd built a group of friends who shared my values, more or less. Continuing the process of coming out, my ex-wife and I decided it was time to tell the kids. It took a long time for me to work up the courage. They were still fairly young and I knew there would be some explaining to do. However, I knew they didn't have the same perception or baggage I had added to the issue.

I walked into my oldest daughter's room. At 10 years old Caity already acted like a little adult. She had just gotten off the phone with a friend when I said, "Hi, baby. Can I talk to you?" My daughter doesn't handle surprises well. I could see the panic sweep across her face. "No, no. It's OK," I said calmly and smiled. "No big deal. I just wanted to talk to you about something real quick. No one died and no one's in trouble."

"Then what is it?" she asked.

Based on conversations and comments I'd heard her make over the last several months, I assumed she had figured out my "secret," so I thought this conversation would be a quick, let-me-confirm-what-you-already-know information session. "Well, I don't think you'll be surprised by this," I said casually, "but I wanted to tell you that I'm gay."

Caity burst into tears. I was taken completely off guard. My confidence dwindled and I felt my admission became more of a confession of failure. I wrapped my arms around her and held her close, letting her tears soak my shirt as I tried to calm her down. After a minute or so I asked, "Why are you crying?"

Still sobbing she said, "I don't know!" I called her mom into the room so we could talk to her together. I also knew her mom could offer her more emotional support.

"Your mother already knows. Your aunts know. Nothing's changed. I'm the same person and absolutely nothing is going to change in your life."

"I don't know what this means," she said. Her mom explained how some men are attracted to other men like women are attracted men and vice versa. Caity took in the words and we watched her put the pieces together in her brain. I was shocked to find out she didn't know any of this. She began to calm down. "Well, does Abel know?" she asked with concern.

"Uh, yes," I said, "Abel knows." I smiled slightly and Caity and I hugged. "I love you, baby."

"I love you, too." Within a matter of minutes she was back to her old self and it was as if our conversation never happened, at least for her.

I felt like a failure. Her pain was all my fault. Why couldn't I have been born straight? Why couldn't I have made the marriage work? I ruined any chance of my kids having a normal life. *They probably won't even be able to maintain a marriage without it ending in divorce*, I thought, berating myself further. Maybe I'd given up too soon. Whatever negative thing happens in their lives will be a result of me not being able to make it, I concluded.

It was another two months before I worked up the courage to tell my younger daughter. Emma, then nine, and whose nickname is G, sat on the family room couch the day after Christmas. This time her mom and I approached her together.

"G," I said tentatively. She had just gotten a new laptop for Christmas and most of her attention was focused on online games.

"What?" she said, clearly annoyed at the distraction.

"Your mom and I have something to tell you. Can you close your laptop for a minute?"

She sighed, obviously irritated by our inconsiderate disruption.

"I don't know if you knew this or not," I said nervously, "but I wanted you to know that I'm gay."

She clutched her laptop, jumped up off the couch and shouted, "What?! I'm leaving! And I'm taking my laptop with me." Her mom and I laughed out loud.

"Do you know what that means?" her mother asked her.

"Yes, I know what it means. He likes guys," she answered confidently. There was a brief pause. "Does Abel know?"

Whatever apprehension I had was gone. "Yes, Abel knows," I said. "He's gay, too." She seemed more shocked to hear about Abel being gay than me. "Do you have any questions, or anything else you want to know?"

"Yes," she said matter-of-factly. "Taylor Lautner. Do you think he's cute?" We laughed and I gave her a hug. Soon Emma was back playing her games and seldom brought up the topic again. This coming out process went much better than the last one and, with my family in the know and firmly in my corner, I decided I needed to tell my parents. Moreover, at some point I was afraid the girls would bring it up during a visit and I would have some explaining to do. It was better if they heard it from me than caught wind of it from someone else.

Coming out to my parents felt defiant on many levels: against them, against God and even against my very nature. But after I met Abel I knew he was going to be around for a while and they needed to know who he was. It was late Saturday afternoon when I made the phone call, following a pep talk from my ex-wife to go through with it.

"Hi, Mom," I said.

"What's up?" My mom always sounds excited to hear from me when I call. My mouth was dry. At the same time I knew what I had to do and the time felt right.

"I need to tell you something. I'm gay." I just said it. "I've been in the process of coming out for a long time. I know when I was in the ministry we taught you that this was somehow your fault, but it's not. It's not anyone's fault." I went on to quote research that I'd read about how the incidence of homosexuality was found to be higher in women who were particularly fertile. It turned out that my mother fit in that category.

"Well, I have to be honest with you," she said. "I already knew. I Googled your name and saw you were part of a gay man's professional group."

I guess I forgot to set my profile to private.

"I love you," she assured me.

To this day I have no idea why my mother was Googling my name.

"I love you, too," I told her. Never one to fail me, my mom was always in my corner. I didn't know what, if any, impact this would have on her after all these years. It had taken me a lot longer to get to this place than she or my father did, and I was aware that things weren't going to just be OK with them overnight. "Would you like to tell Dad, or would you like me to do it?" I asked.

"Uh, I think you need to do this. Hang on. I'll get him." This one was going to be a little more difficult because my father is particularly religious and lives the Gospel doctrine according to the law with which he was taught.

"Hi Pop, I just wanted to tell you that I'm gay. I don't want you to hear it from someone else. I love you and I know how you feel about it, but it is what it is." I was already committed to getting it off my chest so I just said it. I'm sure it wasn't the call he expected that afternoon.

"Well," he said, "I'll tell you what I told you years ago when you sat in my living room: I love you and I will always love you no matter what you do. But, you know the Bible says it's sin and I'll pray for you. We won't bring this up again."

I knew what he said was said in love, with perhaps a little fear and exasperation in the moment, but it rubbed me the wrong way. It felt like the Bible was being used to hit me over the head with yet another message that I was a failure. I was done with being ashamed of who I was, but more than anything, I was just tired. I was tired of running, tired of pretending and tired of acting.

"No," I said abruptly, "we *will* talk about it and I'm not going to go around pretending like it doesn't exist. I disagree that it is a sin. What I learned at Love in Action was wrong. I love you, too, but I'm not hiding this."

I felt angry, but unclear if that anger was directed at my father or his belief system.

My father's tone softened. "OK. I love you." Our conversation was short. The tsunami inside had reached its peak and, with my last important confession, began to finally diffuse. I felt relieved and exposed all at once. All that remained was unrecognizable emotional debris waiting to be cleaned, put back in place, reorganized, or discarded.

There was so much. Where would I start? What would I do with years of self-protection? Anger, disappointment and disillusionment left me feeling vulnerable. Then there was still that nagging question of why am I here? What purpose do I have? I stood in my room for a moment, collecting my thoughts before going back into the family room to report what happened.

"So, how did it go?" my ex-wife asked. I was visibly shaken.

"Fine," I told her. "I got the usual crap from my dad about how God could change me." I went on a rant. "Who does he think he's talking to? I dedicated over 30 years of my life to this and it simply doesn't work. He has the audacity to tell me what God can do when he's never lived this. He doesn't know what it's like. His platitudes mean nothing." In fact, all those pithy clichés in which I once found comfort became meaningless, if not hurtful. God was *not* in control, His ways were *not* higher than my ways and the Bible was nothing more than empty promises.

It all led to nothingness. A book, which once united and bound me to my parents, now tore us apart. I pitied them. They were wrong, believing empty words and holding to archaic, unsubstantiated claims, which were historically inaccurate and contradictory. I washed my hands of their religion and further indoctrinated myself in secular research and intellectualism.

In our conversations Abel seemed to side more with my parents' point of view than mine. It angered me. If there was any contention between us, it frequently revolved around religion. "I just don't understand how you can believe that crap," I'd tell him.

"First of all, American Christianity is not historical Christianity. I don't agree with your parents' cultural interpretation of the Bible. Their doctrine comes from their church experience, but that doesn't mean Christianity is not true," he'd say.

"Also," he would often add, "there is a difference between truth and belief. Belief can't be proven; it's just what we *think* to be true." It took me a long time to grasp this concept. As far as my emotional response toward religion, I didn't care. The intellectual side of me, however, was intrigued and I thought of all the applications of this concept to education. Why we are the way we are had more to do with belief and perception than truth. I would revisit this later. For now, I needed to focus on understanding my life only with what I *knew* to be true.

Festinger, L. (1957). *A Theory of Cognitive Dissonance*, California: Stanford University Press.

– 9 –

Resuming Life

SHORTLY AFTER ABEL and I started dating, he asked me to get an HIV test. I refused. I was terrified at the thought of contracting the disease and I simply didn't want to know. Living in denial was easier than dealing with the possible reality of having a "gay disease." HIV would be the crowning event in a life shrouded by the shame of being gay in the first place. I had been cautious in my activities and stayed away from higher risked behaviors. Nevertheless, I was overwhelmed with fear at the thought of being tested. My mind raced with what-if scenarios.

One thought was noticeably missing: What if God allowed me to get HIV because of my sin? The God of the Bible, that I believed in for so many years, that ruled my thoughts and punished my sinful behaviors, was finally gone. Whatever consequences, if there were any, were purely as a result of my own behavior. It was cause and effect science. That thought in and of itself was freeing. I didn't realize how much my "faith" entrapped me in ridiculous fears of retribution from God and the shame of failing him. My life, if I wanted to achieve anything, would be the result of deliberate choices and actions. That said, if I had the disease, there was no one to blame but me.

After weeks of arguing with Abel over his request, I found the courage to drive to the clinic, just outside the gay district of Sacramento. I certainly wasn't there willingly, but he was clear: "If you want to have a relationship with me, you'll get tested."

The building was nondescript with just a small sign on the front door. Only two people occupied the multi-office suite. The surroundings of used office furniture, peeling paint, and dated computers reminded me of my time at Love in Action. You take what you can get to keep a non-profit running. *The irony*, I thought. *I'm sitting in a gay non-profit waiting to be tested for HIV after all those years of preaching against it.* I wondered if people there were gay. I wondered if they were HIV-positive and I wondered if the same passion drove them to work for almost nothing because they believed in their cause like I believed in mine. None of those mental acrobatics kept my mind off of the real reason why I was there in the first place.

The office was quiet. The only activity was the person in the back room assisting someone who had come in before me. My heart and head raced down the track of the worst-case scenario, telling my kids I'd contracted a disease and knowing it would be years before they'd understand what it was and how I got it.

I began self-reflecting. Why was I so driven to be loved that I'd have sex with almost anyone? How could I have let myself go so far down a path that, logically, I knew was like playing Russian roulette? I was a good person, a moral person. I was trustworthy and tried so hard to be an example to my children. I wouldn't want that lifestyle for them. In fact, I'd feel like a failure as a father if they did what I did.

I'd been so harsh on gay people who'd contracted HIV. I seldom said it out loud, but the thought was there. *I'd never do that! You deserve what you get. The gay community only raises money for HIV because of their self-centered, immoral lifestyle.* It all looked so different now. My anxiety began to get the best of me and my stomach started to turn.

"Tim? You can come back now," the voice said, rattling me out of my thoughts. He introduced himself, but I couldn't remember his name. I forced a smile and followed him into the back.

We sat down in a private office with more dated furniture, separated by old office dividers, obviously donated. Some still had not been put together. He shut the door. "I need to ask you a few more questions."

"Sure," I said, trying to hide my nerves.

"If you test positive you have the option of making this information available to the Centers for Disease Control, or keeping it private. What would you like to do?"

The first question sent me into a political tailspin. As a conservative, I believed that *of course* the information should be made available to the Centers for Disease Control. The public has a right to know of the iniquitous carrier of such a horrible disease. But now the disease had a face on it; it was my face.

"You know, I think I'd like to keep it private, actually," I said.

"OK. Now I just have a few specific questions about the types of sexual behavior you've been involved with."

I sheepishly answered his questions. If there were a right way to engage in promiscuity I'd done it, but this entire experience suddenly felt like an out-of-body experience and I was watching the interaction as an observer. I just couldn't wrap my mind around being there, or grasp the consequences of a positive reading.

"Alright, I'm going to put this cotton swab in your mouth to get a sample," he said. "It takes about 20 minutes to get the results back." My mouth was dry, but he was able to get what he needed.

I waited in the reception area anxiously anticipating an answer. Part of me returned to the familiar depression and thought, *This could be my way out. I'll die of AIDS and all this pain will come to an end once and for all. The perfect end to a tragic, purposeless life.*

"Tim?" the voice said again. This time I was prepared for him. "Come on back and we can discuss the results." My legs were weak as I stood up.

"Your results were negative," he said, immediately relieving the anxiety I'd nurtured for what seemed like hours. "Let me give you a form with the results for your records and if you have any questions or concerns, feel free to come back and talk to us." With that enormous weight lifted off my shoulders, I floated back to my car to call Abel at work.

"Hey!" I said exuberantly. "I got tested and the test results came back negative. I *don't* have HIV." I expected that this would be the end of the uncomfortable conversation we'd had for several weeks. It wasn't.

"That's great," he said, with less enthusiasm than I showed him. "Will you send me a copy of the results?"

"What?" I was incredulous.

"I'd like to see a copy of the results."

"You don't believe me?"

"No, I believe you. I'd just like to see a copy of it."

I was furious. "You son of a bitch!" I yelled. "Why would I lie to you?! What do you want from me?"

"Look," he said holding his ground. "I don't play with this. You know I don't believe in arguing, but I'll fight you on this. You refused to get tested for so long that now I just want you to prove to me that you did it."

"Fine!" I yelled, along with a number of expletives and name-calling. "I'll email it to you when I get home." I hung up the phone, thinking this was the end of our relationship. I wasn't going to date someone who wouldn't take me at my word."

That night, after he'd received a copy of my results and I'd had a chance to calm down, we talked.

"I love you," he said, "and if the results came back positive, it didn't mean the relationship was over. It just meant things would be different."

I wasn't sure what to make of that statement. This man, with whom I'd been in a relationship for just a short time, said that HIV *wasn't* a deal breaker. He said he'd love me anyway. I knew he was right to do what he did by demanding I get tested. He showed fortitude and held his ground. I was impressed by his character and maturity. He was the person I'd hoped to meet in all of my escapades, just in a much different form than I'd expected.

Neither Abel nor I had experienced the more mainstream gay lifestyle, attending bars and clubs, like everyone hears about. We'd been around it, talked about it, analyzed people in it and wondered what the draw was. Feeling particularly adventurous one Saturday night we decided to go to a popular dance club. We drove downtown for dinner and then walked to the club.

"Is there a charge to get in?" I yelled over the pounding music to the attendant at the door.

"We don't have a cover charge until 9:00," he yelled back.

"Great!" I said, holding my hand out to be stamped. Abel did the same. "How come you don't start charging until 9:00?" I asked the man.

"Because that's when people start to arrive."

"That's just so late," I said to Abel as we walked into the dimly lit, multi-room dance club. Abel agreed. It turned out we were the only ones there.

"You wanna dance?" he asked me. I had never danced in my life. I was a choir director. The only thing I knew to do was sidestep and clap on the offbeat. I was definitely out of my element.

"Uh...you go first. I'll watch," I screamed back. Abel hit the floor before I could finish my sentence. He was like watching a cartoon. He had no inhibition and was there to have a good time. I laughed out loud, though no one could hear me.

"Come on!" he encouraged me. "Just relax and have fun!" He grabbed my hand and pulled me on to the floor. I looked around to see if anyone was watching and started to sweat profusely. My mind flashed back to standing in front of one of my choirs. Step left. Clap. Step right. Clap. The only comfort in the moment was that no one I knew was there to see me.

After a few minutes Abel suggested to we go to the bar and get some waters. "That'll be $5," the bartender shouted.

"For water?!" I said incredulously. "Abel paid the tab and threw in a couple of dollars for a tip. I'd planned to nurse that water all night long at that price.

We went from room to room and experienced the different types of music and atmospheres. Eventually, I relaxed and started having a good time, letting myself dance with abandon and enjoying my time with Abel. A couple of hours later we left, just as the crowds started pouring in, and concluded our evening with a nice walk downtown.

As much as I wanted to hold Abel's hand, we were in public. Instead, we just walked close to each other. I glanced around from time to time to make sure no one was watching or that we weren't about to get beat up. I wouldn't have thought twice about holding someone's hand if we had been straight. It was a simple act of love, but I didn't feel I could do it in public.

I had fun at the club. Dancing, which had been described to me growing up as a predecessor to sex, ended up to be more like exercise. I enjoyed watching people and the club was a vast change of pace from my otherwise suburban life. We decided to go again the following weekend. This time we'd meet one of Abel's friends there from school.

Shawnda was a single mom in her 40s who had a number of children from as many fathers. Some of her kids were in their mid- to-late 20s. Abel was drawn to her sense of humor and the two of them agreed that meeting at the gay club was a good idea. I was worried what she would think of Abel and me, especially because of the age difference between us. I felt self-conscious about meeting her, let alone letting her watch me dance.

It was apparent right away that Shawnda had had a rough life. It was significantly different than mine and yet similar in other ways. Nothing about her suggested that she judged me. The age difference, race difference and even social economic differences between us didn't matter. We danced, laughed and had a great time that night, sitting outside with our bottles of water, watching people and listening in to "private" conversations.

"Dude, I'm looking for a pair of sunglasses that look kind of like these," said one of the patrons holding up a similar pair of glasses. The three of us stared at him, wondering why he brought sunglasses to a nightclub in the first place.

"You are very attractive," he said to me, locking his eyes with mine. "I mean, I'm straight, but you are a very attractive guy." I didn't know what to make of his comment.

"Thank you?" I hesitated.

"Well, listen, if you see glasses like these, but white, they belong to me," Then, as quickly as he came, he left, moving to the next table.

Abel beamed, knowing my struggle with self-image. "See? Even the straight guy thinks you're cute."

"He was high," I said, dismissing his comments. We laughed, eventually making our way back to the dance floor. Still, the compliment wasn't lost on me. It was the affirmation I still felt like I needed. It was comforting to know, however, that I had someone to go home with, without the worry of contracting a disease. As we left the club that night, I saw the guy smoking outside. I was glad to be through with the hookups. I was also glad to know the character of the person I was with, and that his habits were more in line with mine.

We spent the next two weekends at the club. Feeling a bit more adventurous, Abel had heard of shots that taste like chocolate cake batter. The taste of alcohol is atrocious to both of us, but cake batter! That was just too alluring to pass up.

"OK," the bartender explained, "take the shot and then immediately follow it up by putting this lime in your mouth!"

"We'll need two limes," Abel said. "We're going to share this." Confused as to how two people would share such a small amount of liquor, the bartender handed Abel a second lime. Abel quickly downed his half and handed the glass to me. I quickly downed my half and shoved the lime wedge in my mouth.

"Wow!" we both exclaimed. "It *does* taste like cake batter."

"That'll be ten dollars." The bartender reached out his hand.

"Here you go," Abel said, reaching into his pocket to pay.

"Ten dollars!" I said aloud. I was shocked. "That would buy a lot of cake batter *and* we wouldn't have to worry about the alcohol." Abel agreed. We left the club for the last time that night, mutually deciding that our party days, all four them, had ended.

Our relationship seemed perfect on so many levels, yet I couldn't get over the differences that plagued me. In his circle of friends I am the oldest person there. I wondered what they thought of me. I had finally accepted my sexuality, but was consumed with appearances. I couldn't be "normal" in the straight community, but thought if I could find someone my own age perhaps I could be "normal" in the gay community. That was my line of reasoning. Blending in seemed to be the best way to achieve acceptance. It was that mental conflict that eventually led me to break up with Abel, at least briefly. It wasn't long before I realized he was too much of a good thing to leave behind.

Abel had already proven he was wise well beyond his years. He simultaneously embodied the maturity of a man twice his age with the playfulness of a boy half his age. He grew up fast, coming from an immigrant family and having to take care of his siblings while their parents disappeared for two years to find work. His commitment to our relationship was inspiring.

Abel and I talked a lot about the future. I was working toward becoming a public speaker, though I wasn't exactly sure what I would be speaking about. Corporate training had been my life for several years. I enjoyed training people and watching the lights turn on as they learned something new, but the topics weren't exactly life changing. I wanted more, but could only dream in a box that excluded anything to do with my past.

My resume was filled with awkward gaps. I had no history before 1997, after removing music ministry, my time as a pastor, Love in Action and Youth for Christ. Whatever the future looked like it would have to be without a meaningful chunk of my life. I wrestled constantly to find a new passion, one based on intellect and non-church experience.

Part of the Sacramento's Speakers Group, I attended meetings month after month and listened to people talk about their passions from helping the elderly to accounting services to advice for working moms. I honed in on my training skills and eventually came up with the company name, Corporate Kindergarten. The name was unique and made people smile. The idea is based on the fact that people's personalities don't change much after the ages of five or six. Effective training, therefore, should be created around basic human behaviors, keeping our personalities in mind.

Abel inspired me to write my first book, which I'd toyed with writing for over five years. *Everything I Learned About Management I Learned from Having a Kindergartner* fit nicely in my plan to host leadership and management classes according to the Corporate Kindergarten model. It was an accomplishment for me to sit down long enough to write, especially since I'd never been much of a reader. The process gave me direction, but not much purpose.

Another passion Abel and I shared was neurology. The subject fit well into our chosen fields, his psychology and mine education. I bought a CD set of 30 lectures by Jeanette Norden, a neurology professor at Vanderbilt University. I had boiled everything down to science and the brain being central to how the human body feels, thinks, sees, perceives and learns. It is capable of producing emotions based on a belief system even in the absence of evidence. I had experienced that firsthand in the Church. If I could figure out how I let my brain do this to me, I would make sure it wouldn't happen again.

The lessons led me to something unexpected. Professor Norden explained, "With all that we know about the brain we still can't explain consciousness" (2007). She said that scientists can see where a thought triggers a movement, but studies are showing that the movement happens nanoseconds before the thought, almost as if the movement were predestined. Whether or not God existed, there was compelling evidence that led me to believe that there was something greater out there.

Whatever consciousness is, I pondered, *it would have to have a much broader understanding of the intricacies of being human than the God of the Bible I believed in.* Even with all of the ambivalent feelings I had about God, I left myself open to the possibilities of a God, or a consciousness, or something beyond my human understanding. What it was, was open to interpretation.

Around this time, I was in for another sweeping change. My girls' mother, who had initially come to stay with me for six months and had now been living with me for over five years, told me she was pregnant. She and her boyfriend were having a baby. I didn't now how that was going to work out for them, but I knew she had to leave. The thought of my children, once again, living in two homes was devastating. My younger daughter, G, felt the most impact. She felt betrayed by her mother. G and I cried together as I tried to assure her that the reason for the new baby most certainly was not because her mother thought G wasn't good enough. I took comfort in the fact that the girls were older and better able to understand what was going on. I was glad that we could talk through our emotions, but it didn't change the situation. I was losing them again and they were going into a new living arrangement neither they, nor I, wanted. I didn't want to be alone again.

With a spare room now available, and Abel's living situation somewhat unstable, I asked him to move in. We both had reservations about how this might work, but I only felt comfortable if he had his own room, especially when the girls were home. He brought a calm stability to our lives and the girls liked him. With the uncertainty of a new baby and their mother's relationship with her boyfriend, Abel and I created a reassuring environment for the girls.

Within a few months everyone settled into his or her new roles, but it wasn't until a year later that we learned Abel could cook. *That* was a welcome revelation for all of us, especially the girls, who were tired of my same three dishes. The four of us were turning into a family. It wasn't very far off from what I thought families should look like, except of course for the obvious gender swap of the other partner.

I was glad to be out of the rat race of hookups, searching for someone new, and trying to fit into a mainstream community. In an odd twist of fate, it seemed I found the only other person in the gay community who was as conservative, if not more so, than me. He is committed, monogamous, family-focused, driven to succeed, passionate about education and, if that weren't enough, can make me belly laugh. For all practical purposes, Abel and I became the couple I'd always wanted to be a part of.

Soon Abel became a member of our family, accepted by my parents, and adored by my sister and her family. The more time we spent with my parents the more I began to see the similarities between Abel and my father: both were raised by poor migrant workers, both struggled through their educations in order to support their families, both were outgoing and both were quick on their feet. Perhaps Abel wasn't the one with daddy issues after all, we joked.

My father enjoyed discussing the Bible with Abel. They would often go into another room and start a conversation about faith. I worked diligently to avoid getting caught in their conversations. The whole topic still made me angry.

"You know he doesn't think for a minute that you're a real Christian," I'd always assure Abel when we'd leave their home.

"What do you mean?" he'd ask. "Your dad and I have really good conversations."

"I know you do, but he's an evangelical. To us," I'd use air quotes, "*your kind* are not really Christians. He's praying for your salvation and hoping that through his witness you'll actually come to know Jesus and leave your sinful ways behind." I honestly didn't know how bitter I sounded until Abel pointed it out.

I was completely shocked the day my father asked Abel to pray over the food when we were there one afternoon. *Certainly, he's going to pray again when Abel's done*, I thought. *Otherwise, the food will be unclean. This has to be a joke.*

Over the next three years I watched my father go from "we'll never speak of this again" to embracing Abel and all-too-willing to have a discussion about the harder facts of science and faith. If a voice was raised, it was always mine. If a fight was to be started, I was the instigator. My father handled himself with grace, tact and love. I grew closer with my parents in spite of our differences on the topic of God, religion and some more subtle political ideologies.

At Abel's coaxing I sought counseling to work on our relationship. I was struggling with what it looked like to everyone else for me to be in a relationship with a man. It had nothing to do with what God thought of it as much as what I thought society thought of it. Affection was only shown in the privacy of our home, away from other people.

"How much do you feel your religion plays into your ability to create intimacy with Abel?" the counselor asked.

"That's in the past," I said. The look on my face must have told her differently.

"Really?!" She sat back in her chair. "So you don't think it has any influence on your relationship now?"

"Maybe. But I don't think it has that big of an influence. I don't think much about it."

For the next few sessions we talked about the dreaded feelings: the ones I cut off to make life bearable, the ones that were tied to music, which were tied to God.

"Tim, do you realize every time we talk about God your expression changes?"

I hadn't.

"You get very angry," she told me.

I thought I was done with that anger, but it lay just below the surface of every conversation, every encounter, and any mention of going to church. Other than anger, I didn't feel much of anything as it related to God.

Somewhere along the way I worked up the courage to pull my keyboard out of the closet and play again, mostly at Christmas, or if I heard a song on the radio I wanted to play along with. Occasionally, I got the bug to "play like a black man," as my former pastor called it. It felt good. After all those years, it still brought emotion; emotion that was familiar, but now unidentifiable, unexplainable. Fortunately, it was also easy to turn off.

The counseling yielded no tangible results. So I hated God. I guess I knew that deep down, but didn't see the impact on my life or relationships. Mostly, though, I struggled to find my true passion. I was certainly happy that I had come out. Psychologically, I felt more grounded because I wasn't hiding anything. I felt more available to my kids and more understanding of others. Purpose, however, still eluded me.

"Hey, how would you feel about speaking at the Toastmasters' event at Sac State University?" Abel asked. His friend was the president and they were looking for outside speakers. "Just send him your bio and they will put you on the calendar." It sounded like fun, though I thought these speakers-in-training would probably shred me. I'd picked up some bad habits along the way. Either way, I'm all about education, even if it's using me as an example of what *not* to do.

I sat at my computer to put together an appropriate bio. It should have been mindless. Instead, I found myself traveling back through time. I remembered schools, universities, churches, the travel, and the fun. I remembered the passion, the feeling that I was a part of something bigger than myself. Years earlier I'd ripped up the list of engagements I once meticulously kept. Now my life felt more like a consolation prize.

All things do *not* work together for good. Things just happen, I decided. Nothing is connected. People live their lives and do what feels right to them. How life got here and why humans feel driven to answer why we're here remained a mystery. Under that scenario, homosexuality made sense. It is part of nature in many species of mammals, including humans. It is not sinful, it cannot be changed, it just is what it is. The simplest things seemed to send my thoughts down rabbit trails I just didn't understand.

I'd created my Facebook account, like most of America, but purposely blocked people from my past. Gradually, however, people would reach out to me, some from the ex-gay ministry. I was too embarrassed to talk to them and kept the conversation away from my personal life as much as possible. Occasionally I'd "like" something on their walls, but I didn't want anyone to know that I ultimately failed as an ex-gay. My relationship status still showed single and I never posted pictures of Abel and me together.

I was shocked when one of my married ex-gay friends contacted me and asked, "Have you heard about John Smid? Apparently, he's having a change of heart. We had lunch and he sounds completely different. He asked about you and said he'd really like to talk to you."

I was suspicious of Smiddy, but mostly because I was suspicious of ex-gay ministry. I knew people were sincere, but they were sincerely wrong. I wasn't sure what to make of this information. Smiddy and I hadn't talked in years. I had a bitter taste in my mouth about how my time at the ministry ended, though I couldn't remember the exact details. I'd heard that he had resigned his position at the ministry and I looked him up on the Internet.

I found his new ministry site, GraceRivers.com, and read several of his blogs. John danced around the issue of whether or not homosexuality was a sin. Until he was ready to admit he was wrong, I would have nothing to do with him. Telling people homosexuality is a sin is an oppressive statement and I would never put myself in that situation again. Still, I was intrigued by John's changing position.

Smiddy, though a kind man with a great sense of humor, was always steadfast in his beliefs and made it clear where he stood. Grace was secondary to toeing the line. He'd come up with some crazy ideas about God toward the end of my time with him in the ministry, but he was convinced he was doing the right thing. I may not have agreed, but I respected his position.

Love in Action had become the focal point of a documentary titled, "This Is What Love In Action Looks Like," which chronicled the story of a 16-year-old boy sent to the ministry by his parents against his will to be "cured" of his homosexuality. Morgan Fox, the documentary director, first began to film the protests outside of Love in Action's live-in house. Eventually he met John face to face and requested an interview. Over time, the two developed a friendship, finding that their conversations led to openness and honesty that John had not experienced before. He knew, after all of his years in ministry, that a person's orientation didn't really change and the dishonesty about that fact was wearing on him.

It was early in 2012 when I learned that John and Morgan would be appearing on CNN's Starting Point. I was more than a little curious to hear John's perspective. Surprisingly, the show struck a nerve. Seeing John again, after all those years, drew me back to the positive experiences we had working together. I really did like him and, though I didn't know what to make of his new position, I asked our mutual friend to give John my phone number and he called.

"Tim, I first really want to apologize for how our relationship ended." His apology was heartfelt and sincere. "I made a big mistake and the ministry was never the same after you left. You brought something to the ministry with your music and your gifts that we never had again. It felt like a piece of the ministry was just gone."

His words, though I appreciated them, weren't as meaningful as was the fact that we were talking for the first time in 16 years. I missed John. I missed our friendship. I missed the evolution of our lives. I regretted that I had cut him off through my divorce, the birth of my children, and the darkest, most difficult days of my life. Yet, it felt like time stood still and we picked up where we left off. John and I talked for three hours.

Mostly, I felt I could be open with him about where I was in my journey, with the questions, the anger and the lack of resolution. He didn't judge me. In fact, he was more vulnerable than I had ever known him to be. It was disarming. I longed for a conversation with someone who understood my journey, someone from my past. I wasn't completely honest, but that was because I didn't know myself well enough to know all the damage that had been done, or the pain yet to be uncovered. Our conversation was the first step toward a healing process yet to happen.

Norden, Jeanette, Understanding the Brain, The Great Courses, The Teaching Company, 2007

— 10 —

LETTING GO

JOHN AND I continued renewing our relationship and I watched his position about God and homosexuality evolve. In many ways we were on the same path, but his was more complicated because he was still married. I worried about his wife and what this would mean for her. John was working on his new book at the time and sent me a copy to read. I'd talked to John about publishing the book for him. With my business book out I'd briefly entertained the idea of publishing other books as a business venture, but when it came right down to it, his book dealt with issues I wasn't ready to address. I tried to read it, but just didn't have the mental strength to think about anything related to being ex-gay. I didn't want to get sucked back into the argument about whether or not homosexuality was OK, stale arguments over the interpretation of Scripture and mostly, face the pain from which I'd finally escaped. I made excuses for avoiding the topic. After all, I'd honed the art of avoidance when life became too difficult.

John connected me with other Facebook friends, such as Michael Bussee, the original founder of Exodus International. Michael was one of those people the ministry taught us was an apostate and we should avoid. He had fallen in love with someone in the Exodus ministry shortly after Exodus started, changed his view and has since spent his life trying to reverse the affects of the organization he began.

I had also reconnected with John Paulk. Up to that point I only had brief contact with him after Love in Action had moved to Memphis. He and Anne went to work for Focus on the Family and started Love Won Out, which proliferated the ex-gay message around the world with much more financial backing than Love in Action could give them.

Occasionally, I'd Google John Paulk's name to see what was happening with him. I knew he'd left the movement ten years earlier and started his own catering business. The gay community kept a close eye on John, even years after his involvement. They blamed him and Anne for keeping the idea of being "ex-gay" alive, and for subsequent on-going political showdowns from the Christian right. They were ruthless in their attacks on John and Anne. I understood why gay people didn't like their message, but the venom with which they came after these sweet people was uncalled for, in my opinion. Accusations of how John and Anne were profiting from their message, which activists presumed was the only reason they gave it, were ridiculous.

Now John and I shared a private online conversation. He told me that things had changed between Anne and him. He, like so many of us, was in the process of coming out. I had no judgment, only empathy for him as he walked through the beginning stages of divorce. He, like I, has children. I knew the pain all too well. I related with John's struggle. There was so much at stake for him as he, unlike me, had to do it all publicly. I couldn't imagine.

I was simultaneously drawn to, and repulsed by, topics around ex-ex-gay, gay Christians, and an era that, for me, was long gone and mostly forgotten. Gradually, like looking at the neighbors through a peephole in the fence, I started reading posts by other ex-ex-gays, primarily people I knew, like John, and wondered what had happened to them. Ambivalent feelings left me tense, though I didn't know why. Soon, I'd either close my laptop and sigh, "Who cares?!" or just surf on to something else.

Online one night I saw a post John Smid made on one of Michael Bussee's pages. I wanted to respond, but it required me to join that particular group. Reluctantly, I filled out my information. The fact that John and Michael were on the same page was odd to me. John had strong opinions about Michael and people like him, in the past, who "turned their backs on God." I couldn't quite wrap my brain around the newfound friendship. Whatever comment John had made evoked enough of an emotional response in me that I felt the need to say something.

The posts I read from other members of the group bothered me. They complained and whined about how terrible ministry leaders had been to them, about how the Church had done them wrong, and how society oppressed and abused them. I don't like victims, or the victim mentality. Besides, I presumed, I had already dealt with this idea of ex-gay and ex-ex-gay. I certainly didn't need a group of melodramatic blamers to make me feel better about myself. I wasn't even sure why I was there.

I sent a private message to Michael:

...I don't normally join groups based on my sexual orientation. I have gay and straight friends and sexual orientation is a non-issue. My comment was simply that I don't feel like a victim or a "survivor"....I take issue with the words survivor and victim because I feel we are personally responsible for our actions...

Michael graciously explained that many people in the group did not all go through the ex-gay programs willingly, or "rationally" in their quests to fix what they thought, or were told, was broken. Michael's words gave me a little more compassion for the people that needed his help, but I was not one of them. I had no ill will toward anyone. I made a rational decision to join the ex-gay community when I was younger. I didn't need a support group now.

Quickly, I retreated back to my life away from the past, turning off any feelings or thoughts I had. Facebook, once again, became my platform for sharing witty quips and funny stories. As past friends from the ministry started reconnecting with me, I made sure my profile was set to reflect a successful Tim, who had overcome adversities, maintained a sense of humor and was living the good life. Slowly, with each renewed connection, came feelings and memories that again captured my thoughts. My mind felt invaded, often sending me into a daydream of past events with unidentifiable emotions.

I soon began drifting into a deep depression. I was certainly used to the ebb and flow of the feelings of worthlessness, but this was much deeper. Abel's presence alone helped alleviate the depth and longevity of the depression over the last few years, but this time I couldn't shake it. Thoughts of suicide once again took their grip. I struggled to work. Making the kids' lunches for school seemed like an insurmountable task. I drifted through my days waiting for those feelings to go away, but they didn't.

What was becoming painfully clear is that I lacked direction and meaning. Those renewed connections brought me back to the days of focus and clarity, working toward something that was bigger than me. My years of corporate training gave me something to do and I was making good money at it, but I wasn't happy. I'd even begun working with teachers of adult basic education and social workers, involving myself in issues of education and the workforce. It's not that it wasn't a good and worthy cause, but I was operating off of pure intellect and, as much as I tried to force it, my heart wasn't in it. It was, as Solomon said, all meaningless (Ecclesiastes 1:2).

Through John Smid, I learned that Lisa Ling, from the Oprah Winfrey Network, was doing a piece on ex-gay ministries. The network set up a meeting between Exodus International's director, Alan Chambers, and several people who had gone through an ex-gay ministry, but found no change. These people wanted to confront Alan about the damage Exodus International was doing. At this point, with all of the reconnections I'd made, and knowing some of the people this report was about, I was curious.

Abel and I snuggled up on the couch to watch the show, like we do most weekends, as news and documentary junkies. We psychoanalyze people, often pausing the show, or muting during commercials to discuss our "findings." I'm not sure if this is what happens in other houses with two social science majors, but our inner-nerds peak on the weekends. I expected this show would be no different. Neither of us was prepared for the flood of emotions that was about to decimate my analytical brain.

As Lisa Ling initially gave context to the ex-gay movement and showcased a new convert, I felt a lump in my throat. I remembered so well feeling hopeless, broken, unworthy, unlovable, trapped, unable to move forward, and useless. Like the young man on TV, I envisioned being married with children, fitting into a heterosexual society. Belonging. Unlike him, I had a history of experience in the

Church and believed it was the answer. He only hoped it was the answer. To divert my emotions, I paused the show under the context of explaining to Abel the history behind people or comments. I really just needed to breathe.

"Can you relate to his story?" Abel asked at one point. He could sense my emotion, in spite of what I thought was well-rehearsed stoicism. The fact that he noticed meant I also had to acknowledge it. I knew a verbal response would unleash a flood of tears I didn't think I could stop. So I nodded, and redirected Abel's attention back to the television.

The stories of formerly married men with children were all too familiar. I had been fortunate. My ex-wife didn't humiliate me, or keep me from my kids. The fact that she left me for someone else was a blessing in disguise because the focus of problems were taken off me and put on her. These guys faced the full brunt of losing families, friends and their church communities. Their pain was profound.

Watching Alan Chamber's reaction to these men and women as they shared their stories was, in a strange way, vindication for me. I knew he wasn't responsible for my journey. In fact, when I met Alan, he was the guy who made the announcements at the Exodus Conferences, not the Executive Director. Quite frankly, I was surprised Alan became the Executive Director. I hadn't talked with him in years, so I'm not even sure how it happened. Yet, here he was compassionately listening to these stories – my story – and gave a heartfelt apology for all the pain the message of Exodus International had brought.

I sat silently as the show ended, deciding if I should allow myself to feel the immense pain of this journey or, like I had for the last twenty years, make a joke and change the subject. Two decades of changing the subject had taken its toll. I was tired of being angry, tired of keeping up the façade, and tired of stuffing emotions. Tears began streaming down my face. The floodgate was opened and I didn't know when it would end. Abel sat with me, quietly, while I cried.

For twenty years I had faced my journey alone. I held so much shame and self-blame for being gay, for losing my marriage, for failing as a minister, failing as an ex-gay, and failing as a Christian. I hid in embarrassment, not realizing that others, former friends, had similar journeys. I kept starting over with new relationships and presenting only what I wanted people to see. I had no history. No one in my circle knew me for more than a few years, except for my family, in whom I never confided.

I'd earned degrees, written a book, and started a company with almost no passion. My endeavors were intellectually challenging, but devoid of emotion. Writing blogs about subjects for which I had little interest was exhausting. It was a rat race and I was losing. My life was crashing in on me and now I was forced to admit it. I knew the task ahead was messy, but clear: I needed to reconcile my faith, emotions, experiences and intellect. I wanted to be one person. That job seemed insurmountable in the moment.

I'd been in the process of writing a new book on education and business, but abruptly cancelled interviews with people and gave no explanation why. I disappeared off social media and deleted information off of my LinkedIn account. I suddenly didn't know who I was, what I did, what I believed, or how to relate to people. The carefully crafted persona I'd created didn't have fears, anxieties, or mistakes. He was confident, creative, intellectual, smart, funny and successful. The only problem is that he wasn't real. Perhaps others saw through it, but the strategically constructed barrier kept me from finding out if they did.

The darkness of the depression kept caving in on me. I'd seen a lot of counselors in the past, but none of them made much headway. It's possible I just wasn't ready to hear it, but more probable I was completely unaware of how disjointed my life had become. Paying someone to listen to me talk felt self-defeating; I was too much of a loser to have friends who would listen to me talk for free.

Fortunately, along my intellectual journey to understand the brain I'd heard of cognitive behavioral therapy, CBT, which addresses the underlying causes of emotions and feelings. CBT offers practical ways to address problems like depression and anxiety. The holistic approach of combining intellect and emotions appealed to me. Either way, I was open to almost anything that would put a stop to the pain.

I searched online for a therapist knowing that at least one criterion was that he was straight. I still had little connection to the gay community and I was more interested in someone who shared my values as a parent than someone who shared my sexual orientation. I randomly picked someone on the list and sent an email, which all but begged for help.

"I need to let you know, I'm not gay," he responded, "but I think I can help you."

"Oh, good!" I responded back. "To be fair you should know that our source of disagreement is more likely political than sexual orientation." I assumed he was a screaming liberal, as my past experience with psychologists dictated.

Part of the problem I had with fitting in anywhere was feeling like I didn't belong: too liberal for conservatives, too conservative for liberals, too straight for gays and too gay for straights. Really, though, I was too ashamed to be me. I hated myself.

In our first session I knew I was in the right place. My new therapist was able to keep up with my disjointed intellectual ramblings and ambivalent emotions. "Slow down," he'd often say. "What are you feeling as you say that?" I didn't know I was feeling anything. My story had become just a tale, someone else's journey, a time in history in which I was an observer. To claim it as my own was to admit defeat. I felt I was all of the things I'd been running from, a colossal disappointment. Now, I began to sort truth from my own fiction.

Therapy provided enough courage to do the unthinkable and reach out to friends with whom I'd had no contact in almost a decade. I was hungry for history. "I know it's been a long time," I wrote in my email, "but I've missed you and thought about you often." I'd known these particular friends since I was 18. No one knew me or had been through more with me, than these two. I didn't know how they would react to my new life or my partner, but my emotional crash brought me to a place of feeling like I had nothing else to lose.

"First off is thank you," read their response. "We really miss you. Our times together with you were some of the best memories [we] have." Our friendship picked up where it left off. Their lives, like mine, took unexpected twists and turns. They, too, were forced to re-evaluate what they believed and why; they also came to different conclusions than their Pentecostal faith dictated. Our biggest regret was that we didn't go through it all together. We didn't have each other to rely on through some of the most significant changes in our lives. Still, we were together now and it felt good. In one email, I had a history.

I continued making contacts with old friends, some from the ex-gay ministry and some whom I'd met as a pastor. I began feeling empowered enough to do something else I hadn't done in 20 years, publicly talk about my life in the ex-gay movement. I started a new blog using my old TimRymel.com website as a cathartic way to face my shame. This time, I wasn't writing for search engine optimization, or trying to build a following as I did with my business and which had become mentally exhausting. This time I wrote to empty my mind and begin living as one person.

It was a huge risk. I reconnected with friends and pastors, and even people who maintained their position that homosexuality is a sin. I didn't know if they knew I'd come out, but I was well aware of where they stood on the issues. I even knew how they came to their conclusions; I'd felt the same way for years. Would I now be shunned? Ignored? Would they look down on me in pity like I had looked down on others? I felt fragile. Yet, like coming out all over again, I was compelled to be known for who I am. I needed to know if anyone cared.

"I have absolutely NO background to share with you," wrote a friend from Memphis in the comments of one of my blogs, "but I wanted to tell you that I love you no matter what. You are still one of the most talented human beings I've ever met in my whole life and I'll always appreciate you for helping me find my inner black singer."

Her comment not only made me smile, it made me rethink what Christians thought about the issue of homosexuality. More than that, it made me rethink what *I* thought about Christianity.

Something indefinable had been stirring in my soul for a long time. A year and a half earlier Abel and I visited my old church during the Christmas season. It's a mixed congregation with a white pastor and soulful worship, where I used to play keyboards with the band. We made our way to the very back of the church after the service began because I didn't want to be noticed by anyone who might recognize me. As the congregation and choir swayed to the music I stood still, soaking it in like water in a withering field. I didn't want to give Abel the impression I was interested in making this a weekly event, especially since I held so much animosity toward the right-leaning, anti-gay pastor. I'd long since lost most of my ability to sing, but something about the music took me back to a place in which I found solace and strength.

"So you liked it, huh?" Abel asked as we hurriedly left following the benediction.

"It was alright," I shot back. "Why did you think I liked it?"

"Because your eyes had tears in them during the music," he said.

I didn't think he noticed. "I guess so, but I would never go back to a church where I couldn't be me, and the pastor of that church does not like gay people." I changed the subject.

I had been trying to make sense of that feeling I get around Gospel music for a long time, especially in light of what I learned of neuroscience. In fact, I would sometimes reproduce the feeling at the piano and introspectively try to "solve the equation" as to what caused this feeling to exist. Everything had to come down to a biological response to external stimuli. The thought of something spiritual happening in my body was beyond reason and that would make me susceptible to believing a lie. I couldn't take that chance anymore.

Now I was at a different place. Not every feeling needed an explanation. Why I am so moved and inspired by Gospel music is perhaps as inexplicable as why others are moved and stirred by classical music, or the ballet. There is something transcendent in the music that brings tears to my eyes, makes me feel as connected to God as I have always understood him, but without shame or conditions of grace that used to be there. I feel inspired, encouraged and unconditionally loved. It's a warm embrace beyond reason that allows me, for the moment, to rest and trust that, like so many old Gospel songs say, "Everything's gonna be alright."

My friend's comment, "I love you no matter what…," also made me think that perhaps the tide was changing in the evangelical church toward acceptance of gays and lesbians, something I never thought I'd see in my lifetime. My old friends made it clear that they accepted my partner and me, even admitting, "I've always wondered if it was an issue with God. I know we made a big deal about it in the Church." Abel told me I always assumed the worst of people when it came to the issue of whether or not they would accept me as I am. Years of experience told me I was being realistic, but perhaps only of a largely bygone era.

My friend's simple response had a powerful effect on me. Shame was losing its grip and I was gaining confidence. I remembered the leader of the speaker's group to which I belonged would often say, "Follow your passion. Talk about what you know, embrace your experiences and be yourself. Those people make the best speakers." Those are easier words to say than do when you've spent your life hiding what you know, your experiences and who you are. The five years I'd been in that group was spent chasing every reason I could think of to talk about anything but what I'd been through. That too was beginning to change.

I was happy to share my life with past members of Love in Action, some I'd never met. My blogs are heartfelt and rely heavily on my experiences and feelings in and out of the ministry. To present information outside of that venue, however, was to fully integrate my past into the present. I wasn't simply exposing myself to the people I knew loved me, but opening myself up to be shamed. I watched on the sidelines as John Smid and John Paulk publicly and courageously came to terms with their lives. Sometimes the very people with whom they served in ministry, and who claimed to love them, shamed them. Not only did they live through it, but they seemed to grow deeper in their convictions and characters. They inspired me, as they had years before, by not only living out loud, but expressing deep emotion, admitting when they made mistakes, and most importantly, building more authentic relationships.

One of the most difficult and intellectually challenging parts of this journey was to face my one-dimensional view of God. I had changed, but my view of God had not. I could not imagine God as something other than a Pentecostal-loving, Republican-siding, sexual behavior overlord with rules, regulations and guidelines.

The Church uses phrases like "love the sinner and hate the sin," and defines grace only in the context of sin. It feels good to say that the blood of Jesus covers all of our sins and we're living free, but relationships in the Church belie the underlying tone. We must always be on our toes, ready to capture every impure thought that crosses our mind; dress appropriately; avoid offensive words, which is forever redefined by culture; pray fervently and unceasingly; and if the New Testament missed anything, refer back to select parts of the Old Testament for reference.

Really, I was so angry at a broken system that I, as my liberal Christian friend told me, threw the baby out with the bath water. I could accept none of it.

It turns out I wasn't mad at God at all. I was angry with a culturally devised version of who God is, as defined by a theology and maintained by a religious-political machine. I was wounded by the Church. It wasn't intentional. I went along with it because I didn't know any better. I lived in a sub-subculture of a version of Christianity in which I was raised.

One afternoon I walked into the office of The Very Reverend Dr. Brian Baker at Trinity Cathedral Church in Sacramento. My therapist referred me to him. Walking through the doors to meet an Episcopalian minister meant either I had completely backslidden from the faith and there was no hope of return, or I'd finally come to a place of openness and I was willing to look for answers in unsuspecting places.

"I have one question," I said bluntly as I sat down in his office. "How do you know that Christianity is true? Answer this and I'll leave." He and I laughed, knowing this was a question of the centuries. He probably thought we were going to be in his office for a very long time.

I had watched Dr. Baker's video on "Jesus and the Gays" where he explains how Evangelical Christians came to their conclusion that homosexuality is sin. He explained all six Scriptures in the Bible related to the topic and gave cultural context. Having argued against such pro-gay theology I was quite familiar with those passages. His style, however, was disarming. The fact that he is a straight man who shows compassion for members of the gay community was intriguing. I had to meet him and learn more.

"I didn't grow up in church," he told me. "I only attended services when I was at WestPoint Academy because of a pretty young lady I was interested in."

"Obtaining a Ph.D. in theology is quite a commitment," I remarked.

"Well, over time my interest grew," he said, "I can't really say I was a Christian even in school, but I was learning about God with an open mind."

"Then why Christianity?" I asked.

"Because it's in my DNA." Dr. Baker went on to tell the story of meeting a Buddhist monk who had just come out of three years of silence. He was impressed with the religious man's sense of peace and closeness with God, as he understood him. "I thought, I want what that man has," he said. "And then I realized that I would have to completely change my DNA to get it. That monk was enveloped in a culture, a thought pattern and a belief system that is completely different than mine. I understand God from the standpoint of Christianity and He makes sense to me. That's my DNA."

For the first time in 15 years, God now made sense to me. The culture of Christianity, in which I grew up, was how my family understood and grasped the concept of God. It's a culture that was passed on to me. The music that stirs my soul creates a connection that draws me near. The most incredible part of this is that it not only transcends culture, it speaks to us *in* our culture, where we are and how we understand life. It doesn't ask us to conform to something we can't comprehend, but meets us where we are, exactly the way we are. Those are the fundamentals of teaching. Find out who your audience is and tailor your message to reach them. God is much bigger than I ever thought He was.

We like the thought that God would reach out to man in his own culture in a way that he understands, but we can't stand the thought that God would not change him into a politically right-leaning, anti-abortion, anti-gay marriage legalist. Grace is given freely, we reason, but it must be maintained by behavior.

I cannot change my sexual orientation. Would I prefer to live as a heterosexual in a heterosexual society? Absolutely. Life is easier. I could hold hands with the person I love in public without worrying about what people think, or worse, being beaten up. I would have gotten to fall in love when I was a teenager, and discovered what it was like to connect with someone at the level I didn't know existed until I was in my 40s. I would like to know what it is to grow up with "normal" problems, without the baggage of hiding a shameful secret for which I would be judged and condemned to hell though I had no control over it. I probably would have lived my life in the Church in stride, never questioning, always believing my world view was the only world view, and the world was going to hell in a hand basket because of gay people, liberal politicians and rogue judges. That life was never mine to have, though God knows I gave it my best shot.

Some people say I gave up and they can cite others who have made it work, or at least appear to have made it work. I did give up, at least initially, but that was until I learned to let go of preconceived ideas, theology, cultural views, explanations, anger, disappointment, bitterness and "supposed to's." Life is *supposed to* be this way. God is *supposed to* do this for me. I'm *supposed to* have achieved this by now. And the list goes on.

Giving up is easier than letting go, but it leaves people bitter. It's an admission of failure. When a person already feels like a failure, giving up isn't that far of a stretch. Letting go, however, requires courage, thought, uncertainty and faith. We wonder: If I let go of the bitterness, what will occupy my time? How will I relate to the world around me? More importantly, will anyone catch me when I fall? The answer is yes.

─ II ─
SELF-ACCEPTANCE

LEARNING TO ACCEPT oneself is not an exclusively gay problem. My children are teenagers now and some days it seems like they've taken a big step backwards on the quest to discover who they are. When they were younger they marveled at their own artwork, handwriting, singing, and dancing. Today they're more realistic about what they can and can't do. Like the rest of us, some days they feel great about themselves and other days they crumble, wondering what's wrong with them.

Those of us who grew up gay in church experienced this, too, but with the added stress of hiding how we truly felt, or guarding the occasional slip of the tongue that gave away our shameful secret. When the other kids in youth group got to point out someone from the opposite sex to whom they were attracted, we had to sit silently, or lie. If we couldn't tell the truth to others, how could we tell the truth to ourselves?

The lies I told to get by in the straight world became such a part of my life that I believed them myself. I'm a bold communicator in business, but when it came to personal relationships and creating intimacy, I said what I thought the other person wanted to hear without any regard to whether or not it's what I felt. I believed I was telling the truth. The only inclination I wasn't being honest was the anxiety that gripped my mind with ferocious fervor. Years of counseling and medication made no difference.

I loved my wife, but couldn't fess up to the fact that a huge emotional wall separated us. I was not wired to be in a relationship with her on that intimate of a level. I said and did all the right things, but there was no feeling behind it. No matter how much I prayed or believed that I just had to fake my devotion until it became real, didn't change the truth. She knew it. I couldn't bring myself to admit it, or even say it out loud, until the day she was moving out. At that point, it only confirmed what she already knew: I was a gay man trying to live up to an ideal that simply wasn't true.

Honesty in the Church is not the virtue we like to pretend it is. As human beings we have discriminating thoughts, feelings of disgust and anger, hatred toward people we love or don't know, and sexual lusts and fantasies of all varieties. These thoughts and feelings do not preclude the Christian community. Often, Christians sit in judgment of people who live open and honest lives, all the while hiding their own humanness. The result is secret lives of behavior, which judges, condemns, finger-points and creates self-righteous pundits disconnected from humanity at large. Why? To protect a religious representation of a perception of God.

When we don't measure up to these ideals, we think there is something wrong with us. God is not happy with us so we drive our feelings deeper underground, afraid to be human and afraid to be honest. It's difficult to accept oneself when all of the mental and religious social cues tell us we're not good enough the way we are.

Ryan Andresen is one example of many. A Boy Scout who met the requirement to become an Eagle Scout, Andresen was denied his award because he is openly gay (Bennett-Smith, 2013). Had he lied or remained silent about his sexual orientation, he would have received his Eagle Scout award and the Christian world would be none-the-wiser. He would have been pointed to as an example of achievement by the religious right. He would have been considered a "success" story the way I was of the ex-gay movement. Instead, he gave up the accolades and the title to tell the truth. Naturally, the irony of his duty to "live your life with honesty," part of the Boy Scout Oath, is rather glaring. More value is placed on silent deceit than absolute authenticity.

I remained silent for far too long. I know of many others in the ex-gay community who held out a picture they wanted everyone to see regardless of their true experiences. Like me, they also believed their own lie. Not intentionally, but because we either feel responsible for upholding an image of God's power we've been taught *and truly believe*, or we think it's just we who are failing. We don't want to be embarrassed that we can't measure up.

It goes both ways. Examining higher profile marriages in the ex-gay community, I noted that those people are always "on" and under scrutiny. To admit any difficulty in a relationship – and every relationship has difficulties – is seen as a crack in the armor instead of courage to be honest. It's a small wonder any relationship survives, gay or straight, under those circumstances.

Coming to terms with one's sexual identity is the most truthful thing a person can do. To admit it to one's self can be a leap, especially if growing up under the condemning eye of a fundamentalist denomination. To openly live that life is another leap entirely. For me, that meant living above the shame.

On my journey I'm learning to be honest about how I feel. It's important to note these statements are in the present tense. This book is not about a journey completed from which I espouse pious lessons learned for others to follow. It's about accepting my humanness as it is and learning to relate it to the world around me. That means sometimes painfully stating feelings, which may alienate me from the people I love. Self-acceptance requires an inventory of who we are, what we believe, and how we feel.

I once told Abel I was not physically attracted to him. Fortunately, Abel has enough confidence for both of us and it often carries our relationship. He's not cocky, he's secure. A loaded statement, like the one I made, sometimes rips relationships apart. He was able to understand that I love him and he could separate my issues from his.

As we calmly talked through my confession something unexpected happened. My feelings toward him began to soften. The separation we felt, because I wasn't talking, began to disappear and I was drawn into an intimate connection, based on total, if not ruthless, honesty. In true Abel fashion he lovingly looked me in the eye and said, "You wanna hold my ugly-ass hand?"

Becoming honest with others and myself has also meant letting go of "supposed-to's" and accepting what is, what I truly feel. It's a risk that others may not agree with; they may choose to not be in relationship with me. The end result, however, is that people who want to be there with the real me are people with whom I can build real relationships.

In my days of promiscuity, every rejection confirmed that I was unlovable, unwanted and inadequate. I was driven by shame to find *the* person who would tell me otherwise. Like an abused child I made compromises and gave more and more of myself away in the illogical hope that someone would give me value.

My girls have gotten older and naturally begun the social dance of meeting boys and contemplating relationships beyond just the friendship stage. I've listened to my daughter talk about the boys that she's met and "dated," meaning who she's hung out with at school. Sometimes my daughter wonders aloud if she's attractive enough, has the right personality or exudes the confidence the boys she's most interested in are looking for.

"Remember this," I've told her. "There is absolutely nothing wrong with you. You are enough, just the way you are. If a boy is looking for someone who has a different hairstyle, or personality, or bigger breasts, then he is not the right person for you." It's along the lines of what I wished someone told me when I was growing up.

Unfortunately, like so many of us growing up gay in the Church, I was not at a place to look for love. I believed I was unlovable, even to God. I wanted to hear from Him the same message I gave to my daughter. Instead, I heard, "I love you, but..." It was the same message I gave to the lesbians on the radio show 20 years ago in Santa Rosa. I didn't even realize the significance of my words at the time.

It was presumptuous of me to say, "God loves you too much to leave you the way you are," especially knowing now that they couldn't change their sexual orientation any more than I could change mine. I cheapened God's love by putting conditions on it. I nullified the work of the cross by saying if they didn't conform to my interpretation of the Bible, then it didn't apply to them.

American Christianity offers an odd dichotomy when it comes to self-acceptance. On one hand it teaches people to love themselves, and others the way that God loves them, and on the other hand it implies that people are worthless without God. I don't know how many times I've heard people talk about how sinful and terrible they are "except for Christ." What kind of message does that send to people who don't hold the same beliefs? If they don't have Christ, are they too worthless? How can we love all humanity while feeling that our own humanity isn't good enough on its own merit? I have value because I am a human being. My sexual orientation, beliefs and behavior do not detract from my value. Ironically, isn't that also the message of pro-life groups? Would they stand in as much confidence if they knew those babies would grow up to be gay? Would they turn around later and protest those same babies their rights to be human and loved?

In my quest for self-acceptance, I've had to honestly admit that I was not comfortable with homosexuality, not even my own. The term "gay" represented a stereotype in my mind of effeminacy, flamboyance and decadence that left me cold. Like my view of God, these perceptions were practically hardwired. To associate myself with the gay world was unthinkable. I've since come to understand that gay people are as diverse as straight people.

One of my first friends in the gay community was what I'd call a "flaming liberal." If it weren't for his sense of humor I never would have talked to him. His comments were frequently angry and biting. We mostly avoided political topics; however, when it came to one of the presidential elections I passionately made my conservative choice known. He couldn't comprehend how a "self-respecting gay person" could choose anyone besides a Democratic candidate. In spite of my reasons and explanations for fiscal responsibility, along with a plethora of sound arguments, as I saw them, he was not moved. "It's obvious to me," he said, "that your decision is purely self-loathing." He felt I was betraying the gay community.

In some ways he was right, at the time. My political decision was not because I was self-loathing and I would vote the same way today, but his statement forced me to think about how I saw myself as part of the gay community. It wasn't a label I willingly took, or applied. I didn't want to be identified with a culture so diametrically opposed to my conservative beliefs.

Identifying or labeling something "gay" left me unable to accept men who had what I considered less-than masculine traits. I wouldn't acknowledge that I was a sensitive person because I perceived overly sensitive gay men more like junior high girls than men. I saw sensitivity as weak, though I feel deeply. I've since come to recognize some of these traits as neither masculine nor feminine, simply human. These traits more often are strengths, not weaknesses.

I think it would be easier to fit a stereotype. I, as most people, like labels, at least when it comes to others. Labels categorize and compartmentalize people into race, religion, sexual orientation, etc., and help us interact with our version of what that looks like. However, labels also keep us from exploring the complexities of human existence. Labels allow us to make assumptions and judgments. Sometimes they help us find the group with whom we most identify, though that requires us to label ourselves and possibly believe something that isn't true about us.

My oldest daughter, a cheerleader, suspected a former Dallas Cowboy cheerleader was going to become the new coach at her high school. "Is she hot?" I asked.

"What are you?" she shot back, looking confused. "Are you bi?"

"I'm a man." I laughed.

"I know, but are you bi?"

"Why do you need to label me as something?" I inquired.

"I don't know what to think when you make statements like that," she confessed.

A lot of us don't know what to think when we can't neatly and quickly come to a conclusion about the people we meet. We're forced to get to know them, or do the opposite and disassociate from them, and make our own judgments. The truth is that people don't fit neatly into our definitions and categories of race, sexuality, politics, religion and values. For that matter, we don't either and, if we are learning and growing, we are constantly changing.

Many years ago I worked with a man who swore like a sailor. One day he asked me to accompany him on a song he was going to sing at a wedding. I was surprised to learn that the wedding would be held at his mother's church where she, a Pentecostal pastor, would be officiating.

I couldn't figure out how this man, raised in a Christian, Pentecostal home, had no problem using four letter words, in front of God and everybody, without an ounce of guilt or remorse. I assumed he had backslidden and led a secret life his parents knew nothing about. When I got a moment alone with him I asked, "What happened to you?"

"What do you mean?" he said.

"You know…that you used to be a Christian." I could tell by the look on his face that my question offended him.

"I still *am* a Christian. I don't understand why you're asking me this." He said.

He didn't fit my definition of a Christian, one I thought I knew well. I didn't know what to make of his "confession of faith" and lack of outward example. I quickly determined that if his *mother* was the pastor and not his father, then they were a different kind of Pentecostal. I kept our friendship at a distance because he didn't fit neatly into any label I could give him. Honestly, I was too insecure to pursue getting to know him further. It would have required me to question my own beliefs and it was just easier to distance myself.

Of course we know that learning to accept others, especially as part of diversity training, is getting to know them, but it also helps us to know ourselves. I was surprised at how threatened I felt by the mere existence of the gay community. Having biological children not only distanced my experience from many in the community, but it made me think I was better than them. My "straight mannerisms" allowed me to fit into the heterosexual society without being suspected of being gay. Both of those things made me feel "normal." But they also kept me from belonging.

The truth was, I still didn't want to accept being gay, though I had long since acknowledged it. It was the same dichotomous feeling I had as a child that I wanted to stand out to find value, and blend in to be accepted. My value was intrinsic all along; I just couldn't see it.

My acceptance of members of the gay community, especially those who are different than me, has grown as I've accepted me the way I am. I will never meet the mainstream stereotype. I don't decorate. I don't like shopping. I don't understand, nor do I have an interest in, fashion. I am not a Democrat (or a Republican for that matter). I am first and foremost a father, a committed partner and seeker of truth.

In 2013, I decided that there were more people like Abel and me and I needed to find them. To the amusement and playful teasing by some of our friends I created a group on Meetup.com called Conservative Gays and Lesbians. "That's an oxymoron," my friends touted. In less than a week we had 10 members. Many of them, like me, had religious backgrounds, some were formerly married and others simply held more conservative values than the mainstream gay population. One of the members told us, "It took me 40 years to come out of the closet, I wasn't going to go back into one within the gay community because someone didn't agree with my politics."

Much of what kept me, and keeps others, from self-acceptance is shame. Shame is the enemy of self-acceptance. Shame causes us to retreat from relationships. We cover our perceived inadequacies with hyper-masculinity or femininity, humor, anger, distractions such as work, school, social media, affairs, or substance abuse. It is the antithesis of authenticity and the motivator of dishonesty. The journey out of it is to do the opposite of what we want to do, which is to hide from others.

Many of us have been taught that shame is a way to change negative behaviors. Research has shown just the opposite (Weiss, 2014, or anything by Brene Brown). Shame drives behavior underground. We don't need to look much further than high profile politicians and pastors, usually conservatives, who get caught having affairs, using drugs and/or eventually confessing that they are gay. Shame doesn't go away simply because we recognize it, or feel it. It must be confronted.

In 2010 Abel and I attended our first gay pride parade. To be honest, I was expecting somewhat of a peep show. I'd heard how exciting the parades could be and, though I'm not the partying kind, I was curious. We drove to a relatively close Bay Area Regional Transit (BART) station where we parked our car and boarded a train. People wearing costumes of all kinds were on the train with us. No one was dressed provocatively, but it was clear where we were all going.

We arrived early in the morning in San Francisco and the fences that separated the spectators from the participants were still being set up. Abel and I made our way through the growing crowd and found a spot somewhere in the middle of the procession by the fence. I began noticing the audience around us. People from all walks of life and ethnicities came to watch. An Asian family, which appeared to include a mother, father, three children ranging from around ages 3 to 12, and an older grandparent set out a blanket next to us. Based on what I'd seen of these parades on TV I was uncomfortable standing next to children. I wondered if the family knew what kind of parade this was going to be.

The usual vendors pulled carts up and down the streets selling rainbow-colored items like balloons, over-sized sunglasses, cotton candy and an array of benign gadgets and toys. If I didn't know any better, I'd think we were waiting to see a Barnum and Bailey's Circus. That all changed once the parade began.

Dykes on Bikes® started the parade off by blaring down Market Street on motorcycles while baring pierced and mostly sagging breasts to a cheering crowd. It was a shocking show of defiance that said in essence, "We refuse to comply to cultural norms and religious mores." I felt nauseated. I was inside a culture I knew nothing about, but their anger, even amid shouts of joy and laughter, was profound.

Over the next few hours I saw half-naked men dancing on floats, hyper-feminized drag queens, hyper-masculinized lesbians, and some things, like examples of sadomasochism, I wish I could unsee. I couldn't help but look over at the Asian family next to me from time to time. I would have covered my kids' eyes if I were their father. This family took all of this in stride, even buying snow cones like it was just another day at the fair.

Then something else happened. Something that I've never seen on the news about these gay pride parades. In a sea of blue, gay and lesbian firemen and women, and police officers, dressed in uniform, walked the route behind all of the chaos. Behind them young families walked with kids in strollers, or kids walked with their parents. They were people who looked like, well, like regular people. Like me. For the first time since I'd been there all day, I felt proud.

We all react differently to shame. Some people throw it in the faces of those they perceive to be their enemies. Some hide behind it with outrageous behavior so people never really get to know them. Others confront it head on by putting down their guard, opening themselves up to vulnerability and becoming authentic. I can't help but wonder if much of the shocking conduct exhibited to the religious right would go away if the LGBT communities were humanized instead of demonized.

In the early days, while trying to navigate my way through the culture, I asked a friend how he so easily accepted the more colorful characters he encountered. "There is a reason people do what they do," he said. "Who am I to judge them when I don't know what they've been through?" My friend taught me that self-acceptance is the practice of compassion.

It's impossible to show compassion for others when we don't have it for ourselves. I judged a world around me for not keeping moral principles that even I couldn't uphold. I condemned people for behaviors they openly practiced while I participated alone in the dark. How could I possibly have compassion for them when I couldn't forgive myself? Like exorcising a demon, each time I've made a conscious choice to accept others where they are without judgments, I've made an unconscious statement of self-acceptance and practiced compassion.

The weird thing about being a parent, that no one tells you when those sweet little babies are born, is that at least one of your kids will be a smaller version of you. You will go through school all over again, revisit your struggle with math, and feel feelings of isolation and sadness over being the last kid picked for sports. You will be overtaken by memories of childhood experiences, good and bad, that give you the chance you wanted "if you could do it all over again."

In some ways my youngest daughter, G, is my mini-me. She is driven and hard on herself. She feels like her work is never good enough, things are never perfect enough and she is incredibly high strung. This time, I'm watching from the outside. Frequently, my words of encouragement to her are dismissed. My heart aches for her.

I'm struck by the compassion I feel for her, offering her excuses, and telling her to lighten up for the very same things I beat myself up over. I didn't do a lot of living in the moment. Things would always be better tomorrow, I'd tell myself. Tomorrow never came. I lived in the future because I couldn't master the here and now. Practicing self-compassion teaches me to live in the moment and keeps me from tearing myself down for mistakes, or not measuring up to someone else's standard.

In the Church I held myself to ideals that couldn't be achieved. Whether or not they were Biblical ideals is debated, but it was certainly the way I interpreted the Bible. Either way, denying one's humanity is quite different than denying one's desires. I confused the two. Humans are wired for love, belonging, and intimacy. Denying ourselves the fundamentals of psychological well-being isn't spiritual, it's the basis for mental illness. I experienced that firsthand. I can live without pie, but not intimacy.

In the 1970s, when I first realized I was gay, there were no role models of what a gay person looked like. The information age was a few years out and all I knew of life and God was what I learned in the sub-subculture of Pentecostalism. However, the Christian right was a small, fledgling group without the political ties and influence it holds today. For young people in the Church now, their chances of facing and dealing with their homosexual orientation may be similar to mine, but for completely different reasons.

There is a growing, more conservative Christian segment of the gay community, as well as gay-affirming Pentecostal churches (something I still can't wrap my brain around), and plenty of books and information available to people who want to know about being Christian and gay. But there is also plenty of misinformation that abounds in the political Christian right from groups like Focus on the Family and Pat Robertson's The 700 Club. Much of that information, sadly, came from Exodus International ministries like Love in Action from testimonies so many of us gave in print and video still used to this day. I had to threaten a lawsuit against one well-known Christian University that kept posting my testimony on its website nearly 20 years later.

Let me say clearly and emphatically, we were wrong. Longitudinal research clearly shows that there is no change in people's sexual orientation, in spite of the inspiring and heart-wrenching stories you hear. Most of the people in my era of the 1990s have recanted their stories, including the "rock stars" like John Paulk, who married an ex-lesbian and gave over a thousand interviews. We wanted to believe it ourselves, but the mental conflict took its toll in our lives over time and we had to come to terms with our realities. It's painful to watch new stories of young people following in our footsteps with the same message and determined hope in their eyes that they will be different, as if they have tapped into a magical source we didn't know about. They have no idea what they will face 5, 10, 20, or even 30 years from now. No one could have told or prepared me for where I would be today.

Young people growing up in Christian homes are bombarded with teachings in their churches that homosexuality is sinful and changeable, fueled by outspoken members of the Christian right, supported by political activists, and given with expectations to conform. For the kid struggling with same-sex attraction there will be confusion. He will feel that acceptance of his sexual orientation is an affront to God and his faith. He will battle his very nature to be loved, to give love, and to experience the same emotional and physical connection his straight counterparts get to enjoy without the shame. The message from his culture screams acceptance, but the mainstream gay community doesn't offer much of an alternative life that is identifiable and relatable.

Some young people will rebel in desperation, feeling that if they can't be accepted for who they are, they will gravitate towards who they are not, perhaps even descending into a life of promiscuity and substance abuse. It's not what they want, but it numbs the pain of living a life based on a lie.

Others, like me, will follow the plan as outlined for them to the best of their abilities. They will become rigid, dogmatic and judgmental. The mental battle will take its toll, though they will give it their best fight, perhaps getting married and raising children, like so many of us have done before. Over time, they will likely crack, finding it more difficult to maintain the appearance. Perhaps their marriages will end in divorce, or perhaps they will find solace in anonymous sexual encounters and other sources that numb the pain.

The Christian community could dismiss my observations as sour grapes from someone who simply couldn't cut it, but my experiences with the ex-gay community tells me otherwise. Sadly, these are the realities of many people who started with the best of intentions and, like me, ended up going down paths they never intended to go. The pain is difficult to bear and its effects are farther reaching than we would like to believe.

The road to self-acceptance for someone who struggles with same-sex attraction in the Church can be a long, difficult road. The process is convoluted by conflicting internal thoughts and external messages. There is seldom support from the conservative Church to help people accept their sexual orientations, without also unrealistic demands placed on them to give up the idea of falling in love, or committing to a passionless, unfulfilling relationship with the opposite sex. Neither of those alternatives offer the "abundant life" Jesus promised for his followers, which is also touted by the Church as a benefit of the Christian commitment.

Bennett-Smith, Meredith, Ryan Andresen, Gay Scout, Officially Denied Eagle Scout Honors, Huffington Post, 1/10/2013, http://www.huffingtonpost.com/2013/01/10/ryan-andresen-gay-scout-denied-eagle-scout-honors_n_2449013.html

Weiss, Robert, Guilt - Good, Shame - Bad, Psychology Today, January 6, 2014, http://www.psychologytoday.com/blog/love-and-sex-in-the-digital-age/201401/guilt-good-shame-bad.

— 12 —

LOVE, LIFE, AND MEANING

I DIDN'T THROW THE last part of the title of my book into a single chapter because I couldn't think of anything else to write. Love, life, and meaning are all parts of the human journey as we go through life. My story has pieces of each of these along the way. At various times we experience one or the other, or if we're lucky, we experience all of them together. People spend their entire lives looking for meaning and purpose. It seems only the lucky few find it. I've found mine twice.

If I could describe in a single word where life finds me in this journey today, the word is free. I'm free from lying about my sexual orientation, free from trying to please others, and free from condemnation. There is something about taking inventory in our lives and questioning our values and beliefs that unlocks the doors of potential and possibilities. At the time I wrote my first book I touched on this, not knowing the significance of my own words:

> *Along with self-discovery comes the process of self-awareness. Self-awareness is an honest view of what we think, feel, and believe we want out of life, and what we can realistically accomplish. Self-awareness…defines…the type of person we are* (Rymel, 2012).

The process of self-awareness, as I discussed in the last chapter, led me to realize that much of my Christian life was spent living in fear of God's retribution. What if I'm wrong? What if I say the wrong word? What if I believe the wrong thing? I think it's why so many of us read the Bible over and over again to make sure we get it right. We say we're trying to understand God, but we keep squeezing God into the same Scriptures, reading them the same way and getting the same answer. Even after memorizing all those books in the Bible, I couldn't understand why my mind hadn't changed. Why wasn't I any different? Why hadn't the struggle gone away?

True Transformation

Romans 12:2 says "Do not conform to the pattern of this world, but be transformed by the renewing of your mind" (NIV). Transformation comes only when there is conflict. Three things, working together, will cause us to transform: two opposing thoughts (cognitive dissonance), life experience, and critical questioning. Without these three things working together we're simply learning words and phrases. Certainly Scriptures we've read and heard over and over again come to mind when we see a reason to apply them. If a difficult situation arises we usually rely on "…all things work together for the good to them that love God, to them that are called according to his purpose" (Romans 8:28, KJV). Almost everyone knows John 3:16, "For God so loved the world that he gave his one and only Son, that whoever believes in him shall not perish but have eternal life" (NIV). We feel warm and fuzzy when we think that God loves us. But that, in and of itself, does not cause transformation.

For decades I wrestled to reconcile my human experience with an interpretation of the Bible and Christianity that was as much a part of my existence as breathing. To separate my beliefs and faith from whom I was, as a person, seemed impossible. I fought it every step of the way for fear of being wrong, being unloved and, quite frankly, fear of being cast into hell. When the pain was too strong I first compartmentalized my actions and beliefs and then struggled with horrible guilt. Later, I simply disconnected myself from everything I believed. I pointed my finger at the image of God who I thought, if He had not caused the pain had certainly allowed it. In the process, I let go of preconceived notions of what I thought God should be, do, look like, act like. What He owed me.

Unexpectedly, letting God out of the box freed me from my own prison. The possibilities of who God *really* is didn't make Him smaller to me, but bigger. My narrow-minded view as a human being cannot contain God in a doctrine, a theology, a book, a political party, an ideology or a single theory. Capturing God is like a cat chasing a laser of light. It's elusive. Its origins unclear. I can see it exists, but from where it emanates and the way it radiates is beyond my understanding. As an intellectual person, I've reasoned, I should question God's existence. Instead, I see the wonders of God in science, in humanity and in the most unexpected places, such as the kindness of unbelievers, or in people quite different from me.

Genuine Grace

It occurred to me that if my perception of God was wrong, so was my perception of grace. What if God's grace was even greater than I thought it was? What if the ultimate sacrifice of Christ on the cross came with such a force that it actually wiped away the sin of mankind? What if the same power that ripped the curtain in the temple in half had such significance that any barrier between God and man was removed? What if man was free to experience God without walls, without preconceptions, and without conditions? That type of grace is incomprehensible to us. We've been brainwashed into a culture of fear-based theology and doctrine. We've been programmed to believe a "law of grace."

The law of grace taught me that my salvation was given freely by my belief in Christ…*and* New Testament doctrines *and* select Old Testament doctrines *and* reading my Bible *and* praying *and* going to church *and* sharing the Gospel. The list goes on and on. Quite frankly, that kind of grace wouldn't work in any relationship; it's neither grace, nor is it given freely.

"Have you noticed that gay Christians don't seem to have any rules?" a friend of mine asked me after reading some Facebook posts of mutual friends. He, like me, was trying to figure out exactly what gay Christians believe.

I laughed. "Yes, I noticed that, too," I told him. Gay and Christian were two words that didn't belong together, even after I was coming to terms with my sexuality. My friend and I were raised in the Assemblies of God. Right and wrong were clearly defined. In fact, the slogan in most Assembly of God Christian colleges is "sex isn't allowed because it always leads to dancing." Dancing is a sin.

I noticed something else about those gay Christian posts. I noticed that the men and women who took on the label "gay Christian" weren't bogged down in theological debates, didn't participate in endless finger-pointing about who was living right and who wasn't. They, instead, seem to just accept that God loves them, and they embraced all of their own humanness. Many are active in causes of social justice, helping the needy and trying to make the world a better place. It was a refreshing honesty I never saw during my time in the Church. Quite frankly, it made me uncomfortable.

I recently saw a new book advertised about cheapened grace written by a minister to explain how pro-gay theology devalues God's grace. My first thought was: *It's not your grace!* How can anyone presume to know what, or if, there is a line to be crossed that nullifies God's grace? Is God's grace so fragile that humans, by mere action, can tarnish it? Did God forget to cover all the bases when he gave grace? Did he forget to write out a list of what qualified or didn't qualify for grace? In fact, grace *with* conditions is not grace, but legalism.

I want to make it clear that I have not taken on the label of gay Christian. In fact, I haven't taken any label at all and I don't feel the need to do so. I've found something incredibly freeing about living in the uncertainty of faith.

TEST OF TRUST

Dr. Brene Brown released a lecture series entitled, "The Power of Vulnerability" (2012). In her research she found that people who are the most vulnerable, honest with themselves and others, are people who thrive in uncertainty. They don't have all the answers, but take the most risks and tend to live more fulfilled lives. On the other hand, she found that people of faith have the most difficult time with uncertainty. The irony, of course, is that uncertainty is the very definition of faith.

Uncertainty opens the doors and windows of possibility. It practically kicks God out of the box, leaving him undefined, unpredictable and immeasurable. In uncertainty God transcends human consideration, culture and condition. Uncertainty overrides human opinion, epiphany, dogmas and doctrines.

The same, familiar driving force within my soul that has always connected me with God is still there. I've removed the label and the expectations. I simply enjoy the relationship to something much bigger than me. To define it, cheapens it. To label it, places it in a package, which limits my expectations and makes God smaller – He's only capable of doing what *I* think He can do.

Evangelical Christians will have a difficult time with this. I get it. It's a completely different way of looking at and experiencing God. I didn't get here over night. I don't expect people to suddenly change their minds. Looking at things differently feels like we're betraying our Christian beliefs, if not God Himself. Red lights go off. It doesn't feel right. Your mind is flooded with Scriptures and their traditional interpretations, along with the fears of being wrong.

It seems there isn't a conversation in the Church about love and grace without a conversation about sin and hell. We want people to know "God's love," but they sure better know if they don't accept it - in all its beauty - they'll go straight to hell. His love is abounding and His grace knows no end, but rejecting it – as defined by certain doctrine – only leads to eternal damnation and fire. What's more, people must understand it from a limited theological perspective.

My father tells the story of our pastor, when we were involved in the Pentecostal Church of God, coming over to tell him that my mother was no longer allowed to teach Sunday school. She was caught wearing "men's clothing," a pantsuit. My father, the man who taught me that it was OK to question, asked his pastor if he was going to build a fence around the roof of his house. The same Scripture he used to accuse my mother of wearing men's clothing also stated that there must be a fence built around the rooftop of the house.

Through the centuries, Scriptural interpretation has changed, though the love of God has remained consistent. It saddens me to hear people say, "What if I'm wrong," when it comes to simply loving people where they are. Fear-based religion is simply religion. I don't believe God ever intended people live or love in fear.

Living in Love

While I am in love with my partner, love is not as much about falling into it as it is a state of being. My partner is not my "prize" at the end of a race. Love is not simply about having a significant other, nor is having someone to love the cure for a lifetime of brokenness. Loving him, as well as loving others, is something I can do only because of the journey.

Our relationship is like everyone else's. I can't help but chuckle when someone tells me I live a "gay lifestyle" because it looks exactly like the "straight lifestyle" I had when I was married, minus the arguing, tension, emotional disconnection, and strife.

I get up early to make sure everyone has their lunches. Then it's off to take the kids to school, work between going back to pick them up, and then dropping them off at friends' houses, cheer practice, or afterschool activities. There's housework, making dinners, doing dishes, and running errands. When we have free time, it's either spent having dinner with friends, or vegging out in front of the TV. This leaves practically no time to participate in the gay mafia, or pass out fliers to recruit unsuspecting kids into our sinful lifestyle. Quite honestly, if there were time – and these things existed – we are too tired to go.

Like everyone else in a partnership, the relationship I have with Abel is one that we've worked to achieve. The goals I told him I had when we met changed without warning. The feelings I told him I had for him have shifted with the wind. Some days I wanted him to leave and other days I told him I couldn't live without him. I've wanted to be a business owner, an entrepreneur, and then I'd decided to buy a franchise. Some days I drifted into depression without warrant, and other days I couldn't wait to tell him how great my life was. I'm not bipolar, but fluctuated between embracing my past and running from it. It has been a dramatic ride neither he nor I knew we were on. In the process, our love has matured and grown.

My daughter and I were riding in my car one day listening to her iPod. Plugging her iPod into my sound system is as natural as buckling her seat belt at her age. When a song came on by Macklemore she said, "Hey dad, have you heard this one? I really love this song."

The song was "Same Love." I'd casually listened to it before, but hadn't paid much attention to the lyrics. This time something caught my ear:

> *The right wing conservatives think it's a decision, and you can be cured with some treatment and religion. Man-made rewiring of a predisposition* (Ryan Lewis, 2012).

I spent five years of my life getting out that very message. Now here we were, almost 20 years later, and that message is loud and clear. I never imagined it would be repeated in a pop song, nor my teenage daughter would play it for me. I had another surreal moment. They seem to happen a lot more lately.

I thought back to all the traveling, media attention, press releases, newsletters and the many people who carried that message forward for so many years before and after me. It's a message now ingrained in pop culture, but not used as a message of healing and hope as it was intended.

The message is so widespread there are organizations whose full-time purpose is to stop it. They inform others of all the crazy stuff people in the ex-gay movement are still saying and warning would-be inductees of the dangers of the movement as a whole. I didn't think I would be on the other side, but here I am.

I think being a father has changed me. My daughter, Caity, loves people. All people. She loves them where they are, who they are and regardless of what they look like. Ironically, those were the characteristics I wanted to portray to others about God and about the ex-gay message.

I've learned that true love loves someone as if he or she will never change. He may keep his annoying habits. She may be overweight, have pimples, warts, or a limp. Not only are they acceptable, but worth loving completely, unconditionally, and fully because they are alive. That's really the message I wanted to convey all those years ago.

The Church has gotten away from "Love the Lord your God with all your heart and your neighbor as yourself" and replaced it with "save the family and the sanctity of marriage." The call on Christian radio and television has less and less to do with taking care of widows and orphans and more to do with preserving a way of life. The question is not how do we serve the sinner, but how do we keep things comfortable for ourselves? Even discussions around hot button issues are less about people and more about doctrines. When the battle gets too hard the Church retreats into the corner to strategize a new fight, usually involving political means, instead of thinking of ways to love their "enemies."

It's difficult to love people when we see them as an ideology, a false doctrine, or a lifestyle. They cease being people, for whom Christ commanded compassion, and become political fodder, which must be debated, voted on and controlled. We cannot love someone who is perceived as a threat. Love stops being patient and kind and becomes terse and angry, proud, dishonorable, and self-seeking, Without love we keep records of wrong doing, ignore truth, hurt others, distrust motives, and wait for failure. In other words, we become the opposite of how Paul describes love in 1 Corinthians 13:4-7. Furthermore, when we feel threatened, we stop trusting that God is able to take care of us and we defend ourselves.

On March 24, 2014, it was announced, "World Vision's [a humanitarian organization that helps feed and clothe children and their families worldwide] American branch will no longer require its more than 1,100 employees to restrict their sexual activity to marriage between one man and one woman" (Gracey & Weber). The article went on to say that while the policy on monogamy and abstinence outside of marriage remained in place, married gay Christians could be hired to work alongside their heterosexual Christian counterparts.

The Evangelical "Christian" community reacted swiftly, refusing to help feed and clothe 10,000 children and their families (Weiseth, 2014). They would rather let the children starve than work alongside self-identified gay Christians for a common cause. One of the responses to the article that reported the number of sponsorships lost callously said, "Well, we're in agreement that 10,000 kids losing their sponsorships is a terrible consequence. But it's a consequence of World Vision choosing to make that...decision." People – hungry children – became less important than a doctrine. I can't help but imagine how many *more* children and families could have been served had World Vision stayed the course and maintained the integrity of their initial decision to show love over theology.

I bristled at the suggestion that I was homophobic when I was in the ministry. I was around people all the time that struggled with same-sex attraction. I certainly wasn't afraid of them, as the label suggests. Besides, disagreeing with someone didn't make me homophobic, I argued. That was true.

Disagreeing with someone who is gay does not make one homophobic. The question is, on what basis do you disagree? Common arguments include that if gay people were suddenly allowed to marry and have the same rights as heterosexual couples then society would collapse; debauchery would ensue; children wouldn't be safe; more people would be gay; the doors would be wide open to marry anything and everything; and God's judgment would come down on America.

If God hasn't given us a spirit of fear, but of power, love and a sound mind, as 2 Timothy 1:7 suggests, then why is the Church operating in so much fear when it comes to the issue of homosexuality?

Relationships and Reconciliation

Finding purpose a second time in my life has been difficult because it has meant embracing the journey in all its ugliness, perceived failures and humanness. I had to let go of perfection in favor of relationships. I could fail and be rejected, but not trying is worse than failure.

The ex-gay movement gave me a purpose at the time. Certainly, the travel was fun and the media attention was exciting, but those things are activities. I've repeated some of them during my business career. They, by themselves, don't change people's lives or build relationships. Some of the most meaningful experiences I've had didn't occur at outreach events or on a stage. In fact, I've had a difficult time remembering much of those experiences as I've worked on this book. Meaning comes from building authentic relationships, which only happens when we are authentic with ourselves.

John Smid came back to the office one day after a taping of the Jerry Springer show. He had been a guest of the show along with a husband and wife transsexual duo, she a female-to-male and he a male-to-female. "Everyone has a closet and everyone has baggage," one of them said to John. "When you come out of the closet you just bring your baggage with you." John described an unhappy couple, searching for truth.

There are a lot of people searching for truth, carrying their bags with them from one closet to the next, occasionally opening their suitcases to reveal just a little bit of themselves to others. They hope someone will love them and accept them where they are without judgment. It's what we all want.

For nine years my daughters attended a private Christian school. I taught there and got to know the children and their families. Sometimes, sitting in the parking lot waiting for my kids to come out of class I'd watch the children interact. I saw behaviors that indicated signs of sexual identity struggles in some of the boys and wondered, *What will their parents do if they're gay?* I know of one family, a boy who was a close friend of my daughter, who has publicly spoken out against homosexuals. My daughter told me she suspects he is gay. If that is true, my heart hurts for him. My heart breaks for all those caught in a system that denies their human longing for love. I believe God's heart breaks, too.

As an educator, I love watching the lights turn on when someone reaches an understanding of something he or she didn't know before. It's all the better when that understanding heals a relationship, or causes someone to connect with another human being in a meaningful way. There is a disconnect between the Church, of which I was a part for more than 25 years, and the gay community, of which I am a part by default. The two silently collide as sons and daughters, fathers and mothers, friends, uncles and aunts face their own realities. Christians find themselves suddenly faced with trying to reconcile their love for family or friends with their faith.

After years of defending the Gospel, alongside my brothers and sisters in Christ, I now find myself on the defensive. "Your post boils down to 'I have no sexual self-control, so that means no one else does,'" wrote one blogger in response to a comment I made. "Maybe some men are just made of better stuff than you are. If sex is your god, no wonder you failed." It's an odd place to be, receiving attacks from people who don't know me, or my story. It's especially odd to feel attacked by my own people. Perhaps I once spoke in this man's church. Perhaps our paths crossed. He probably would have assumed I was like him, not knowing the internal battle, the sadness or the pain.

I'm not out to evangelize God-fearing Christians and make them gay, as though that were possible, or destroy their theology. My purpose is the same as it was when I was a worship leader, which is to draw people into relationship with their God and with each other. Paul calls this "the ministry of reconciliation" in 2 Corinthians 5:18.

Meaningful relationships are deeper than the emotional highs I cherished in the Church. They are not camp meeting experiences. Those seldom last.

Significant relationships require thought, compromise, soul-searching and a commitment to love through the fear, the pain and the doubt. These relationships are soulful relationships that lift up humanity in all of its authenticity. We accept the parts we cannot change, embrace our imperfections, and seek to understand others. In doing so, we come to a fuller understanding of God, love, life and meaning.

Brown, Brene, The Power of Vulnerability: Teachings on Authenticity, Connection and Courage. Sounds True Publishing, 2012

Gracey, Celeste, Weber, Jeremy, World Vision: Why We're Hiring Gay Christians in Same-Sex Marriages, Christianity Today, March 24, 2014, http://www.christianitytoday.com/ct/2014/march-web-only/world-vision-why-hiring-gay-christians-same-sex-marriage.html

Rymel, Tim, Everything I Learned About Management I Learned from Having a Kindergartner, CK Publishing, 2012

Weiseth, Nish, Ten Thousand Kids, Deeper, Story, April 3, 2014, http://nishweiseth.com/blog/2014/4/ten-thousand-kids

― 13 ―

CONVICTION, COMPROMISE AND COMPASSION

I RESPONDED TO A blog on a Christian website, praising the writer for keeping the conversation going and admonishing her to take other people's experiences at face value. I shared a little of my story. Someone responded to me with this:

Christ gave you his life, maybe you can give Him your all, take up your cross, and make Him the real king of your life – instead of a relationship that He deems is sinful, when you are hurting Him. We all have things that are hard to not do. Many people decide to not fight it, many people say it's just who they are, etc... Jesus says He will give you the strength to fight, and the Spirit will be with you. He said to go and sin no more. Yes, He loves you very much, but if you choose an earthly relationship over a relationship with Him, that is your choice – and unfortunately, you are creating a wall between you and Him. He loves you more than your partner. Don't put Him second.

In essence, she's saying, "You're just not trying hard enough," and in the few minutes it took her to write her thoughts she dismissed decades of struggle, with just a handful of words, in a single paragraph. Did she think the light would suddenly turn on for me and I would say, "You're right! Why didn't I think of that?!"

Years after my divorce I told my ex-wife I never understood how she so quickly moved on. She said, "I had already emotionally disconnected from our marriage. In my mind our relationship was over long before I met the other person. I didn't just wake up and decide to be with someone else. I had already gone through a painful separation process."

The Church is still in love with the idea that homosexuality fits neatly in a black and white Biblical context. The answer, to someone who has never gone through the struggle, is simple. It's so easy to see. The Bible is clear and the discussion is over. Like my ex-wife, I did not come to the place I am today lightly. There were decades of tears and torment, especially for someone like me who has always tried to "do the right thing."

The pithy statement churchgoers like to make, "compassion without compromise," is a misnomer. It ends the discussion before it starts. It assumes, like the lady who responded to my post, that the Church is right and everyone else is wrong. It doesn't require any deep thought, nor does it take people's experiences into account. It's answering a question that hasn't been asked yet; solving an equation without knowing the problem.

Try taking that "compassion without compromise" approach with your significant other. "I'm so sorry you feel the way you do, but I'm not willing to change how I see your situation. I'm right and you're wrong. I feel bad for you, but that's just how things are." Now put yourself in the other person's shoes. That person who professes his or her love for you pities you and then looks down on you because he or she considers you too stupid to see things from the "right" perspective. Do you feel heard? Do you feel loved? Do you feel human?

I met Tony at work around 1991 while I was in the Love in Action live-in program. He wasn't as secretive about his sexual identity as I was about my involvement with ex-gay ministry. When I realized Tony was gay I worked up the courage to talk to him. Besides, with all I'd learned I knew I could help turn his life around. "You know you don't have to be gay," I told him.

"Excuse me?" He was lighting a cigarette and my statement caught him off guard.

"The reason people are gay is because of poor relationships with their fathers or traumas that happened in their lives. It is possible to change," I said with as much compassion as I could muster. And I meant it.

"Um." He looked confused. "I had a great relationship with my dad. Unfortunately, he died when I was a teenager. We used to play sports together and I helped him in our family business. He knew I was gay. He didn't care. He loved me anyway."

"Well, *something* must have gone wrong," I insisted. "Think back. What do you think happened to you?"

"Nothing happened to me," Tony said. He was clearly irritated with my insinuation that the relationship with his father wasn't like he said it was. "Listen, no offense, but I hope you find what you're looking for. I'm happy the way I am."

I walked away feeling pity for Tony. *Obviously*, he didn't know what he was talking about. He was suppressing memories and was in so much pain even he didn't know it. As long as I was right and

Tony was wrong, there was no reason to have a discussion. I could show compassion without compromise…without thinking, without questioning what I believed to be true, without coming to different conclusions, without making Tony human and accepting his experiences at face value.

When I posted my blog on the topic of compromise someone said, "I'm not going to give up my position of Biblical authority on this issue." That's when I realized that the word "compromise" is a hot button in the conservative church. It means, at least to this person, throwing in the towel and giving up the foundation of their faith. Either the Bible, exactly the way it is believed, preached, taught, and accepted in the culture of the conservative church, is all right, or all wrong. To even suggest a compromise, which by the way is merely talking about how we love people, is blasphemous and there is nothing left to talk about.

A friend, who is a former ex-gay and has since become an atheist, said, "Sometimes I feel more like a Christian now than when I *was* a Christian because I have more compassion for people." He said he no longer operates within a set of preconceived ideals and beliefs. He looks at people as people. There is no judgment on their actions or attitudes and he is able to accept them as they are.

What About the Bible?

Perhaps one thing noticeably missing from this book is an argument over the six Scriptures most often used to prove homosexuality is a sin and condemn gay people to hell: Genesis 19:5, Leviticus 18:22 & 20:13, Romans 1:26-27, 1 Corinthians 6:9-10, and 1 Timothy 1:9-10. As I mentioned in previous pages, I know these passages well. I've taught them and I've preached against pro-gay theology. So how could I simply dismiss these passages and risk my eternal soul, some may ask?

First of all, these passages, like much of the Bible, are up for interpretation. Scholars much more knowledgeable than I, and most people reading this book, have come to opposite conclusions. Throwing my opinion into the ring is not going to change anyone's mind. The interpretations of these Scriptures have done little more than divide sides, create animosity and dehumanize a segment of the population. God, in my opinion, is more concerned about building relationships than destroying them.

Secondly, the word "homosexual" does not even appear in any literature until 1869, when, interestingly enough, it was used in a German pamphlet arguing *against* anti-sodomy laws (Endres, u.d.). The American Evangelical Church, as it is today and which drives much of the current political atmosphere surrounding the topic of gay rights, didn't come into existence until the 1730's (Bebbington, 1993). Humans and human behavior predates Scripture, which by any account, only goes back 6,000 years. I came to the conclusion that the Evangelical Church does not have a corner market on Scriptural interpretation and did not for centuries.

In Sunday school I learned how we humans are fearfully and wonderfully made (Psalm 139:14). That concept escaped me until I studied how we learn. Think of the human body like a box, which contains the five senses we use to experience the world around us. Everything that we learn, believe, and think happens to us in our boxes. We are shaped and molded by our upbringing, the people we encounter along the way, and the feelings we assign to each of those experiences as they happen.

Our biology also shapes our boxes. The DNA we receive from our ancestors programs our behaviors. Our culture and traditions teach us to think in specific terms, as well as determine "appropriate" responses to the world around us. No one can put a percentage on biological influence, but most scientists agree that it is significant.

As an educator I've had to come up with clever ways to present material to diverse audiences. There are often language or cultural barriers and, more often, simply perception barriers. An example of a perception barrier is using the color red, which is offensive to one group of people, while another group of people barely notice its existence. Why do those perception barriers exist? Because I'm speaking from my box - my culture, my perceptions and my beliefs - to theirs.

God is transcendent, above and beyond the boxes from which we experience the world. If you think of it in those terms, there are over seven billion boxes of perception in this world and billions who were here before. This, according to my simple understanding, is God's design. We are each given a sliver of a much bigger picture and can only understand a fraction of that because we are finite beings.

Human connection requires us to work at making relationships with people and we are programmed to do so. We *need* to feel loved, exactly the way we are, accepted, included and connected. We don't find significance or purpose until our basic physiological and emotional needs are met. That stuff is all Psychology 101.

Additionally, we don't have access to other people's boxes beyond what they tell us. We can transfer information from one box to another, but we will never experience the world as the other person. We don't have access to their biology, nor did we grow up in their culture. We can only relate to others based on mutually shared experiences. Even then, we understand other's experiences based on our own. Again, our understanding of the world around us is limited. The only way to know with any certainty at all is to connect with as many other humans as we can, which will be limited to our lifetimes. That, in my opinion, is a brilliant design.

It's also important to point out that there is a difference between truth and belief. Truth can be proven, while belief cannot. Truth and belief are not mutually exclusive, yet one can exist without the other. I may believe that the Bible is the inerrant Word of God, but I cannot prove it. Therefore, it falls into the category of belief. I can say that I believe in gravity on earth, but I can also prove it. Gravity, therefore, falls into the category of truth. It may or may not be believed, but its truth cannot be negated and we are all subjected to that truth.

God is well aware of our inability to comprehend all truth. I do not believe, with the human diversity on this planet and so much yet to be learned, that an all-knowing God would condemn people to hell because they could not make sense of His plan. There are millions of people who claim to be Christians, uninfluenced by American cultural Christianity, who have no concept of the Scriptures the way many of us have learned them. I do not discount their experience with God as they understand Him. It would be arrogant of me to do so. I simply accept them as they are. I believe God does, too.

The Evangelical Church, or at least the most outspoken, perpetuates an image of the gay community as nothing more than sexual deviants. It is an archaic stereotype that still believes gay people can turn other people gay, particularly children; homosexuality is synonymous with pedophiles; and that a singular "gay lifestyle" exists. In spite of decades of research to the contrary, many in the conservative church would rather accept the stereotype, which they feel better fits with their interpretation of Scriptures, than take the time to get to know people for themselves.

I recently held a birthday party at my house where all of my worlds collided. My right-wing, Christian parents came with other conservative Christian friends, along with several of our gay friends, one of whom is a Democrat working closely with the California governor. In an almost unheard of scenario these days, the room mixed and mingled. I heard laughter and story-sharing, and watched genuine human interaction. The following day, when my mother called, I had to ask, "So, what did you think of the party last night?"

"Oh, it was fun!" she said.

"So all of those gay people didn't bother you?" I didn't think it would, since my parents love everyone, but I thought I'd ask.

"Honestly? I couldn't tell who was gay and who wasn't," she said. "It really didn't matter. I just enjoyed talking with people."

The quickest way to destroy stereotypes is to get to know people. Many Christians are often driven, again based on fear, to share the Gospel and present their message of "hope," without listening to human stories. They feel awkward, or guilty if the message doesn't get shared.

At my father's surprise birthday party we asked people to share their experiences about their relationship with my dad. One man stood up to say that he wanted to be like my dad and tell people about Jesus. My father does talk about his faith, but always with love and he's never intrusive. This person was *not* like my father.

"I wear this cross so people will ask me about my faith and then I can share the message of the Gospel."

He should have stopped there.

"If they don't like what I have to say they can just turn the channel. I'm tired of all the liberals and their agendas telling us what we can and cannot say anymore. They're trying to keep us from preaching the Gospel and they want to censure us. Well, I'm going to preach it anyway," he touted.

I leaned over to my friend and cynically added, "And if that doesn't work we'll pass legislation."

Unfortunately, it's people like this that the gay community sees and who are too frequently tolerated by the Church. His message isn't about love, it's about asserting his rights over someone else and feeling that if he doesn't take a stand, the world will be overrun by sin.

The topic of homosexuality in the Church seems to ignite strong feelings that: 1) force Christians to face their own sexuality and 2) cause the Church to believe that if it doesn't do something about the horrific sin of gayness, the world as it is known will come to an end.

CHRISTIANS AND HETEROSEXUALITY

Talking about homosexuality forces Christians to face the fact that they, too, are sexual beings. Naturally, I've had my own issues with sexuality growing up in church, which have now been duly chronicled, but the topic is an important one if the Church is ever going to learn to love a group of people they have defined solely by their sexuality.

In the early 90s I, along with other leaders in ex-gay ministries, met to discuss an approach to reaching gay youth. We wanted to head them off early so they could avoid making the mistakes many of our clients made, leading to drugs, alcohol and promiscuity. Eventually, we came up with a plan to equip youth pastors and church leaders to best deal with youth and homosexuality in the Church. We learned something right away that quickly derailed our message: pastors and church leaders are not comfortable with their own sexuality. In fact, many participate in activities deemed sinful by the church organizations they lead.

According to a report on Internet accountability site CovenantEyes.com, "Regular church attenders are 26% less likely to look at porn than non-attenders, but those self-identified as "fundamentalists" are 91% *more* likely to look at porn" (Gilkerson, 2013). Another survey reported that 77% of Americans view pornography at least once a month (Cardinal Newman Society, 2013). Additionally, one national survey reported that "95% of men and 89% of women said they had masturbated" (Risher, u.d). (We men assume the other 5% of men are lying.) I bring up these statistics because, like the statistic of divorce, human behavior does not respect the bounds of faith. As I stated at the beginning, people are people, are people. The sooner we humanize people the faster we'll reach a state of discussion and compassion.

Sexuality in the Church is either not discussed, or it's discussed only in the context of how sex is *supposed to* work: within the confines of marriage and between a man and a woman. Someone recently told me that in the men's accountability group at his church, he brought up his struggle with same-sex attraction and it shut down the discussion. He was shamed by silence. If the Church cannot comfortably address the topic of human sexuality, it will never be able to address homosexuality, which falls into that category.

By spiritualizing sexuality and placing it in the limited context of the Bible, deciding what is appropriate and inappropriate is easier than muddling through journals of human sexuality. Sexuality, like life, even for people of faith, is messy. If the *supposed to's* don't work, the next best option is to hide the behavior in the dark and never talk about it. The Bible, by the way, provides multiple definitions of families and values, but American Christianity has picked the one it wants.

"I've had hookups outside of my marriage," one ex-gay friend confided in me a few years ago. "My wife doesn't know." He and his family are active members of their church community. No one knows about his extracurricular activity. Chris already went through the ex-gay ministry and is *supposed to* have the answers to his problem. Adultery is the way he deals with the ongoing conflict between his struggle to live a straight life and fight his homosexual identity.

The gay community is done hiding. People would rather not bother themselves with stymied religious traditions that deny part of historical human sexuality. If it means, like Dykes on Bikes, that they have to bare their bodies in defiance and rub Christians' proverbial noses in their eccentric sexual proclivities to make that point, then they will do it, and do it with pride.

Christians and Homosexuality

Naturally, if Christians are afraid of their own sexuality, they are mortified at the thought of homosexuality and its perceived consequences.

As a worship leader I've sung my fair share of songs about the greatness of God. People raise their hands, close their eyes and sing at the top of their lungs. I can't figure out where all that faith goes after they leave the service. I'll admit that I've done it, too. God's greatness is only as big as I feel it is in the moment. When real life kicks in and I feel there's a threat of an infiltration into my way of life, I look to other places for safety, like politics and community. God alone, in my mind, becomes incapable of keeping me safe.

It sounds silly, but there is a dichotomy between what we say we believe about God and the way we show it. What if the Church just loved people? Instead of picketing and handing out tracts and flyers about the evils of abortion and homosexuality there were handshakes and hugs. Compassion. Kindness. Is God big enough to show His love to people with whom we disagree? Is He capable of sustaining our "righteous" way of life without political involvement?

When my ex-wife and I decided to put our kids in public school we were tormented by the "what ifs" of public school. We knew drugs, alcohol, sex and parts of life we'd shielded from them would now be accessible. The decision was difficult, but we felt their new schools offered better academic opportunities. The one thing that gave us confidence was that we raised them with values and gave them the tools they needed to tackle the real world. They have not disappointed us.

Proverbs 22:6 says, "Train up a child in the way he should go: and when he is old, he will not depart from it." If we have to trust our kids – and we do – then why is it so difficult to trust God with the lives of people we don't know, or understand? More than that, can we defend the humanity of people we don't understand?

In 2001 Americans watched in horror as Muslim extremists attacked our country. Most of us didn't know much about the Muslim religion, but our introduction by violence and death certainly didn't make a good first impression. For years, I believed that all Muslims were extremists and I said so. In fact, one friend finally told me that my sweeping generalizations made me sound stupid and uneducated.

The biggest impact on my belief wasn't simply what happened on September 11, 2001, it was the silence of the general Muslim community following the attacks that made me believe they stood in agreement with those vicious terrorists.

There have been bills introduced in a number of states that allow people of faith – particularly the Evangelical Christian community – to refuse service to those they believe are homosexuals, or hold values that offend their religious beliefs. In Uganda, Christian right extremists backed a bill that not only discriminates against homosexuals, but ensures prison sentences and allows for public humiliation. I'd like to believe there are those on the Christian right who take issue with the discrimination and torture of these individuals, but like their silent Muslim counterparts, most remain quiet.

In my years in ministry in the evangelical church I met genuine, loving people. My Facebook friends list consists of people who are pastors, leaders and members of the evangelical community, people with whom I served so closely I considered family. I read their political posts, and mostly agree with their points of view. I get it. Government is too big, special interests have taken over the court system, and morality is shoved down our throats by the liberal media. If we share an opinion that isn't politically correct we're likely to receive backlash, lose a television show, and be mob-lynched by left-leaning journalists.

But when it comes to human rights and human dignity, we're not talking about politics, ideals, theology or doctrine. We're talking about lives, the precious souls of which Christ died to redeem, as many of us have passionately preached. Are these not the same people Jesus stood against his pharisaical counterparts to protect? Did he ever ask or make judgments about their moral choices before he fed, healed or spoke to them? Was he ever concerned about their sexual preferences, practices or politics? The answer is clearly no. Christians have scratched their heads wondering why the LGBT community is so hostile towards them. Sometimes it's not what is said as much as what is not said. So I must ask, how big is your God?

Bebbington, David, W., Evangelicalism in Modern Britain: A history from the 1730's to the 1980's, London, Routledge, http://en.wikipedia.org/wiki/Evangelicalism#cite_ref-Bebb_3-0

Cardinal Newman Society, 77 Percent of Americans View Porn Once a Month, January, 18, 2013, http://www.freerepublic.com/focus/religion/2979722/posts

Endres, Nikolai, The Coinage and Dissemination of the Term, Undated, http://www.glbtq.com/social-sciences/kertbeny_km.html

Gilkerson, Luke, Get the Latest Pornography Statistics, February 19, 2013, http://www.covenanteyes.com/2013/02/19/pornography-statistics/

Risher, Brittany, You Won't Go Blind, Men's Health, undated, http://www.menshealth.com/health/health-and-sexual-benefits-masturbation#

Epilogue

IT'S IMPORTANT FOR me to point out that I have a deep respect for Love in Action's founder, Frank Worthen and his wife Anita. I experienced caring, kind and selfless people who were, and are, genuinely concerned about the emotional, spiritual and physical well-being of the men and women to whom they ministered. Many of the men and women who went through the live-in or Bible study programs had similar experiences with them.

We in the ministry were not driven by fame or money. I made $18,000 a year for each of the years I worked at Love in Action. Frank and Anita have never taken a salary, as far as I know, in the 40+ years they have operated their ministries. Additionally, I saw them serve the poor and feed the hungry. I feel safe in saying that the members and leaders of Exodus International I have known or worked with are also honest and sincere people. Again, I realize there are those who have more sinister reasons for working in this ministry, but I did not meet nor work with them.

Giving an ex-gay message is difficult in a climate that attacks anyone with non-mainstream views. A counselor friend of mine lamented recently about tightening laws in Colorado. His overarching message is sexual wholeness, but he feels the pressure to acquiesce and alter his message in spite of his personal convictions.

I realize I'm treading on thin ice, especially with members of the gay community. My partner and I have tossed around whether or not we think reparative therapy should be made illegal. On one hand, dismal results, including depression, other mental illnesses and substance abuse are compelling reasons to discontinue the practice. On the other hand, our country was founded on religious freedoms. I would not have been dissuaded from trying to change my orientation even if laws were in place at the time. Of note, I am vehemently opposed to reparative therapy of minors.

While religious freedom is important, it comes with responsibility. Perpetuating theological arguments, which dehumanize, subjugate and harm others (e.g., women's suffrage, slavery and segregation), is not religious freedom; it is oppression. Calling it religious freedom does not change what it is. Believing it is religious freedom does not make it true.

The Church has become an enemy of the gay community because of outrageous statements from people like Pat Robertson touting that gay people wear rings so they can give you AIDS when you shake their hands, (Sieczkowski, 2013), and James Dobson of Focus on the Family who proclaimed Sandy Hook's school shooting was God's judgment because of gay marriage, (Bennett-Smith, 2012). When one segment of the Church reaches out, such as World Vision, the overwhelming reaction of the Evangelical Church is disgust and hatred. Even as I've politely contributed to Christian blogs, I've found the responses to be anything but loving.

Pastors have the opportunity to address these issues in their churches by acknowledging statements made from those who supposedly speak for the religious right and, hopefully, correcting them. More importantly, they have the opportunity to reach out directly to gay people in their communities *and their own churches*. It's really about listening with an open mind, considering the idea that there could be another way of looking at something, and acknowledging other people's life experiences.

We will never come to terms on arguments based solely in belief, so we may choose to agree to disagree. Whatever our beliefs, however, we are all driven by the same desires for love, belonging and acceptance. Along those lines, we have to accept people where they are in their journeys. It is possible that many will come to different conclusions 20 years later, but they are on their own journeys. We can only speak from our experiences and our own convictions. We cannot force our way of thinking down someone's throat who is not ready to consume it. The best approach is to love and to serve.

I've heard from many people in the ex-gay community, who have now accepted themselves and their sexual orientations, talk about the positive things that happened to them during their quest for healing. Many friendships were made, relationships healed, and some found a deep sense of spiritual awakening that ultimately led them down a completely different path. I believe we are personally responsible for our choices, though I realize not everyone gets to make educated ones. Like parenting, we can only do the best we can with what we know at the time.

BUT WHAT ABOUT THOSE WHO STILL CLAIM TO BE EX-GAY?

The Journal of Counseling Psychology released a major study in March, 2014. After researching over 1,600 men and women, they found sexual orientation change efforts to be ineffective (Throckmorton, 2014). So why does ex-gay *seemingly* works for some and not others? I know of no males who claim that their sexual orientations were changed, though some remain married and others remain intermittently celibate. Married ex-gay personal friends have confided significant difficulties in their relationships due to their mixed orientation marriages. Their commitments to remain in the marriages are for a variety of reasons. There are no longitudinal studies at 20-30 years that offer qualitative or quantitative data on the topic. I've read stories of men who are openly gay and married to women. They choose to be in monogamous relationships with their wives. All of that said, the term "ex-gay" is inaccurate.

Neither doctrines nor laws can be based on a handful of experiences. Personal conviction on any subject does not make for sound policy. Our decisions *should be*, but seldom are, based on research and facts. The reality is that most people make decisions based on feeling and belief. If we can, as a society, treat each other with respect because of our common humanity, perhaps we can simply settle on mutual compassion for each other's journeys.

Bennett-Smith, Meredith, James Dobson: Connecticut Shooting Linked to Gay Marriage, Huffington Post, December 17, 2012, http://www.huffingtonpost.com/2012/12/17/james-dobson-connecticut-shooting-gay-marriage_n_2318015.html

Sieczkowski, Cavan, Pat Robertson Suggests Gays with AIDS Wears Rings to Cut, Infect Others, Huffington Post, August 27, 2013, http://www.huffingtonpost.com/2013/08/27/pat-robertson-aids-rings_n_3824401.html

Throckmorton, Warren, Major New Study Finds Sexual Orientation Efforts To Be Ineffective, Patheos, May 12, 2014, http://www.patheos.com/blogs/warrenthrockmorton/2014/05/12/major-new-study-finds-sexual-orientation-change-efforts-to-be-ineffective/

CPSIA information can be obtained
at www.ICGtesting.com
Printed in the USA
BVHW041902130920
588710BV00013B/593